The Worst of Football

Nigel Henderson

From brawls to bribery: The ugly side of the beautiful game

Nigel Henderson

A journalist on the sports desk at The Times, Nigel Henderson has also had spells with the Press Association and The Royal Gazette, Bermuda's daily paper.

A connoiseur of ill-timed tackles and goalmouth scrambles, he likes AFC Wimbledon almost as much as he hates franchised football and the group stages of the Champions League. He is the author of *The Worst of Cricket* (also published by Pitch).

ACKNOWLEDGEMENTS

Thanks to Paul Camillin and Roy Chuter at Pitch, Luke Jefford for the design and Kevin Day for the foreword. The book is dedicated to Sue Corbett and Irene Henderson.

The Worst of Football

Nigel Henderson

From brawls to bribery:
The ugly side
of the beautiful game

The Worst of Football
From brawls to bribery:
The ugly side of the beautiful game

© Nigel Henderson

Nigel Henderson has asserted his rights in accordance with the Copyright, Designs and Patents Act 1988 to be identified as the author of this work.

Publishing by:

Pitch Publishing (Brighton) Ltd
10 Beresford Court
Somerhill Road
Hove BN3 1RH
Email: info@pitchpublishing.co.uk
Web: www.pitchpublishing.co.uk

First published 2005.

ISBN 095424606-3

Picture credits:

Empics:
Pages; 11, 39, 63, 169, 195, 221, 247

Getty Images: Pages; 275

Action Images: Pages; 87, 113, 141

Editor: Roy Chuter

Cover and page design:

Luke Jefford & Associates
3 St. George's Place
Brighton
East Sussex
BN1 4GA
Tel: 01273 600639

Printed and bound in Great Britain by Cambridge University Press

Contents

Foreword by Kevin Day

Every time you see a twenty-two player brawl during a live match on TV the commentator will say: "These scenes are disgraceful." He doesn't mean it. Trust me, I know most of them and they will be enjoying it as much as the rest of us. A couple would be happy to join in.

Like all football fans, they might yearn for goals but deep in their hearts they yearn for more – they want punch-ups, flare-ups and cock-ups. They want red cards, red mists and referees who need police protection. I have seen hundreds of Crystal Palace games and presumably therefore, some goals. But it's not them I remember.

I remember our manager punching our reserve goalkeeper on the nose. I remember Brighton's manager sticking two fingers up at Palace fans and waving money in our faces. I remember a game of five penalties, four of them missed, and I remember the eerie silence that followed the almighty crack of Ian Evans's leg being broken by George Best.

I remember a pitch invasion by Palace and Birmingham fans in end-of-season fancy dress and I'm still not proud of laughing when Charlie Chaplin decked the Pink Panther.

I remember as though it was yesterday a referee telling Clive Allen his shot hadn't gone in even though fifteen thousand people had seen it rebound from the stanchion at the back of the net, and I remember a riot at Loftus Road after Clive Allen had scored against us and run the full length of the pitch to share his enjoyment with Palace fans. Mainly for the look of surprise on the face of a police horse, I remember when someone tried to punch it on the ear, and the even bigger look of surprise when someone tried to kiss it better.

They are shocking, but strangely enjoyable memories. My only regret is that I didn't actually witness Palace scoring during a pre-season friendly against Calais while the French goalkeeper was tied to a post by flags.

This book is about those parts of the game that have been officially frowned upon but secretly relished by football fans all over the world. It is a compendium of the dark arts of football, and therefore contains a fair bit of John Fashanu who, incidentally, once told me he always learned the names of referees' children and pets because that bought him two free fouls!

This book is for all those who believe that even the best games of football are made better by dodgy referees, red cards aplenty and a dog on the pitch.

Introduction

Never sent off, never booked, never even, according to legend, spoken to by a referee, Tom Finney was the archetypal Gentleman Footballer. But let's face it: he was in the minority.

Ever since the Middle Ages, when houses and shops were wrecked, high streets trashed and bones galore broken as drunken louts took it as a licence to maim and mangle – and that was just the players – the sport has struggled to shake off its genesis as a mob game; no wonder successive monarchs tried to get their people to focus on archery practice.

So the next time some old fogey tries to regale you with tales of 'Golden Ages' and the 'Corinthian spirit', or some corporate sponger splutters on about 'the beautiful game' in between mouthfuls of his first prawn sandwich of the afternoon, hit him where it hurts with an example from this book, which brings together the worst collection of footballing malevolence, misadventure and madness ever assembled: from the player sent off within 20 seconds of the start of the Christmas Day programme to the chairman-cum-general election candidate who tried to bribe the opposition to help his campaign; from the player who launched a riot with too much keepie-uppie to the referee who stormed off in the middle of a game; from the player who had to be smuggled out of a ground in disguise to the fans who tried to set light to a manager's wife.

What this will prove to him is that football is, and pretty much always has been, more war dance than working man's ballet. It is nasty, brutish and short (not allowing for Fergie time and a fifth-round FA Cup saga featuring Stoke and Bury). A bit like life really.

The worst fouls

The worst fouls

Hacking, the manly practice that combined a stiff tackle with a swift crack across an opponent's shins (or sometimes just the swift crack across the shins), was largely outlawed when its proponents got a sound beating, metaphorically speaking, at the 1863 meeting to decide on the first laws of association football. Outvoted despite warning that elimination of the act would be "bound to bring over a lot of Frenchmen who will beat you with a week's practice", they stormed off in a strop – to create rugby. But when Eddie Gray was half-crippled by a Ron Harris assault on the bottom of his calf early in the 1970 FA Cup final replay between Leeds United and Chelsea, it was a signal that more than 100 years after the split, the spirit of such challenges was alive and well. Jack Charlton, Gray's team-mate, was later able to reflect on the beautiful brutality of Harris's action, which rendered ineffective the man who had run the Chelsea defence ragged in the original tie at Wembley, yet brought barely a whisper of condemnation from the referee. The tackle can now be observed on an inexpensive BBC DVD, but careful manipulation of the remote control is required to watch it in its full glory in slow motion. And this is the big problem when trying to decide whether violent play of past eras ranks comparison with that of today: the action replays are just not available. While the slightest of sly nudges is nowadays recorded and broadcast from every conceivable angle before being regurgitated via a video grab for the next morning's papers, many of the rashest of challenges from days gone by have been lost to a history that relied almost solely on the printed word. Many, but not all.

1

Charlie Thomson
on Harry Hampton
Sunderland v Aston Villa
FA Cup final. Crystal Palace. April 1913

Sunderland and Aston Villa had quite a rivalry going in the 1912-13 season. When they met in the Cup Final, the Wearsiders, their eyes on the double, were leading the First Division, with Villa in hot pursuit. It was not an edifying spectacle. One regional paper sketchwriter afterwards portrayed the match not as football but as "a grim fight", while his cartoonist colleague drew an equally unsubtle picture – the pitch was depicted as a battlefield, the bodies of the vanquished strewn all about. With the Somme still a few years away, this was Culloden replayed – Charlie Thomson, the Sunderland centre-half and captain, was from Prestonpans, and he acted as though England centre-forward Harry Hampton had personally chased Bonnie Prince Charlie over the sea to Skye. The pair indulged in a skirmish that was not for the squeamish, and it came to a head when Thomson crashed into the Englishman with the force of a horde of humiliated Highlanders. When Hampton lashed out with his foot in response, catching Thomson high up the thigh, it seemed as obvious a double dismissal as you could wish to see, but Arthur Adams, the referee, chose to steer clear of confrontation.

Stud Marks

7/10

While Adams had failed to fulfil his duties, the football authorities were not so reluctant to act – Thomson and Hampton were banned for a month at the start of the following season. A subsequent draw against Villa clinched the league title for Sunderland, but the champions were excluded from the next campaign's opener, the Charity Shield match against Southern League winners Plymouth Argyle, because of their conduct at Crystal Palace.

2

Roy Keane
on Alf Inge Haaland
Manchester United v Manchester City
The Premiership. Old Trafford. April 2001

One biography of the Irish midfielder poses a question that attempts to get to the crux of the matter: what, the authors ask, makes Roy Keane tick? Probably, judging by the sheer number of his brushes with football law, it is a small timebomb buried not all that deeply beneath a rather thin skin. One of the many people to set this veritable Semtex in studs on the countdown to an explosion was Alf Inge Haaland. But when, in 1997, the Norwegian, at the time a Leeds player, stood over the Manchester United enforcer and suggested that he was maybe making a little bit more fuss than was strictly necessary about catching his foot in the turf and tearing cruciate ligaments, he could hardly have appreciated that he was lighting a fuse that would take four long years until it was ready to blow. When it did, in this

Manchester derby, Haaland would find that his shin-pads provided little protection from the shrapnel, for Keane leant back, took careful aim and caught his fellow midfielder in a place that was afforded no shielding: his kneecap.

Stud Marks
8/10

Geologists are still locating fossilised remnants of Keane's boot in Haaland's wound. Although Keane didn't wait for David Elleray to locate the red card in his top pocket, that wasn't the end of the matter, the United player's deliberation coming to light a year later when he allowed ghost writer Eamonn Dunphy to act as ventriloquist to his dummy. But each word Dunphy shovelled into his fellow Irishman's mouth led Keane deeper into a pit of trouble. What we can say with some probability is that the native of Cork didn't utter the exact phrase: "I'd waited long enough. I f**king hit him hard. Take that you c***. And don't ever stand over me sneering about false injuries again." No matter: the FA still fined him £150,000 and banned him for five games.

3

A year or so earlier, Johnson's elbow, being swung at the time in the service of Nottingham Forest, had smashed into Santos's face with such force that his nose collapsed in on itself like a prefabricated building caught in the route of a hurricane, and his eye retreated deep into its fractured socket. A titanium plate held things together physically after a five-hour operation, but the French utility player retained his psychological poise only by spending his time on the sidelines investigating legal avenues – despite Johnson's protestations of innocence. Blades manager Neil Warnock stirred the pot with a few ill-chosen remarks, and perhaps naively brought Santos on as a substitute against Johnson's new club, West Brom. Within a minute, Santos had sought out his quarry and clattered through him with such deliberation that it was evident that he had been visualising the moment in its entirety for the intervening months. Off he went; Patrick Suffo joined him for a headbutt; goalkeeper Simon Tracey had already seen red. Rob Ullathorne and Michael Brown then hobbled off the pitch, and with United down to six men, referee Eddie Wolstenholme was forced to abandon the game.

Stud Marks
10/10

The match was written up as "The Battle of Bramall Lane", but Gary Megson, never the most retiring of managers, was determined have the last word, accusing an unnamed member of the home side's staff of encouraging their players to act injured in the knowledge that they could get the game called off. "If we are called back to Sheffield we shall kick off, then walk off the pitch," he ranted. "There will be no replay." He was right; the Football League decided that the result – Albion led 3-0 – should stand.

4 Adoni Goicoexea on Diego Maradona
Athletic Bilbao v Barcelona
La Liga, San Mames, September 1983

If Keane's tackle was a case of revenge served cold, George Santos's assault on Andy Johnson was enacted, culinary speaking, while still warming in the microwave. Norman Hunter may have bitten your leg, but The Butcher of Bilbao, as Goicoexea was known to his enemies – and there were not too many friends – would gnaw it off square at the thighbone and take it home to cook with some fava beans and a nice Chianti. To an opponent, the quick kill of the slaughterhouse would seem infinitely preferable to the drawn-out death one of his tackles could visit upon flesh and bone once he was roused. And roused he was after Bernd Schuster, Barcelona's German midfielder, started milking the approval of the visiting fans after exacting a measure of revenge on Goicoexea for a spat from an earlier game. Ignoring the perpetrator, the Basque defender instead focused on Maradona's squat legs pegging it unsuspectingly towards the Bilbao area, ball at the tip of his toes, in search of Barcelona's fourth goal. He highlighted the Argentinian's ankles as his target. Maradona knew what it felt like – he later likened the impact to "a piece of wood cracking" – but it was only a couple of days later, as he recovered in hospital, that he realised how bad the tackle looked when he saw it replayed on TV.

Stud Marks
5/10

Goicoexea was banned for nine matches for the assault, while the physical scars of his broken ankle and damaged ligaments kept Maradona on the sidelines for three months. By a strange quirk of fate the Argentinian didn't meet his would-be assassin again until nine years later, when he was making his debut for Seville, but the Butcher was by then a man converted, like an abattoir boss who had suddenly seen his former trade from the cow's point of view. Ambling through Bilbao prior to the match, he popped his head into Maradona's hotel, where he greeted Diego like a long-lost brother. The pair chewed the cud for a good few minutes, looking back on better times, but there was one subject that, you could say, they found too hard to tackle.

5

Josimar on Stuart Pearce
England v Brazil
The Rous Cup. Wembley. 1987

Stuart Pearce's tough footballing education on the Sunday morning playing fields of north-west London – he moonlighted in goal under a Scandinavian pseudonym for Dynamo Kingsbury Kiev whilst a semi-professional with Wealdstone – prepared him for most things that could be thrown at him on a football pitch, even when that was a small Brazilian, oblivious to the ball but urged on by some inner purpose that only he could fathom. While Pearce, on his England debut, was entering the 50-50 tackle firmly but fairly, the South American was still on final approach, and when touchdown came, his undercarriage – two sets of studs – slammed on to the parallel runways of the left-back's shins, before skidding to a halt just below the defender's knees. It had John

Barnes, for one, ready to reach for the sick bag. Standing no more than five yards away from the incident, the winger started to signal for the air ambulance, but Pearce barely flinched at what Barnes described as the worst challenge he had ever seen, simply jumping up, brushing himself down and preparing to get on with the job.

Stud Marks

6/10

Josimar, surprisingly, stayed grounded, having to receive treatment for a twisted ankle, yet the incident ranked so low on Pearce's radar that he failed to mention it in his autobiography. And while the left-back's career went from strength to strength, that of Josimar, an unexpected star of the 1986 World Cup, went into freefall, arrests for beating up a policeman and a prostitute (not at the same time), and for cocaine possession, hurrying his decline into oblivion. He was last heard of playing for a small club in Venezuela, where he was running a drinking establishment, the JosiBar.

6

Vinny Jones on Peter Reid
Manchester City v Sheffield United
Division One, Maine Road, January 1991

If art imitates life, as some say it does, it is perhaps appropriate that the football hardman turned Hollywood luvvie should eventually turn up in a movie called *Gone In 60 Seconds*. The film's title referred to the swift work of America's inner-city car-theft gangs, but it could just as easily be a comment on the length of time Jones was likely to spend before incurring the ref's wrath. Whether he was sliding a fictional twisted coathanger through the top of a sporty Mercedes window in a studio in Tinseltown or scything a contorted pattern through an opponent's shins on a Tuesday night in Grimsby Town, Jones always seemed to be only one step away from getting into serious trouble with the authorities. In truth, he did manage to last more than a minute of most games, but in this one, Jones was like a greyhound out of the traps, taking just five seconds to sniff out his midfield rival, the City player-manager, and clatter him to the turf. David Elleray was fishing for his yellow card before the whistle for kick-off had died away. When, shortly after the start of the second half, Jones repeated the offence, he was given the inevitable red.

Stud Marks

7/10

Jones later made plenty of mileage out of the tackle, including it in a medley of mad moments in the stage show he toured round Britain with his partner in crime, Coronation Street love rat Bradley Walsh.

7

Paul Gascoigne on Gary Charles

Tottenham Hotspur v Nottingham Forest

FA Cup final, Wembley, May 1991

Paul Gascoigne's best mate Jimmy Five Bellies may have had a stomach comprising several storeys, but by the time Gazza had finished with him – he used to fire airgun pellets at his bare backside and pay him a fiver every time he hit it – he had practically no arse. Gazza's accuracy in the tackle, however, often left something to be desired – as he openly admits in his autobiography. Revved up in the opening minutes of his first Cup Final, he careered studs-first into Garry Parker's chest, a challenge that should have earned him at least a yellow card. When the caution failed to come, the midfielder threw his own to the wind and lunged at Forest full-back Gary

Charles, who was innocuously drifting towards the Spurs penalty area. Gazza missed the ball completely and took out Charles in the process. It was X-certificate stuff, but the Forest player recovered quickly and was able to watch without his parents' permission as Stuart Pearce slammed the resulting free-kick past Erik Thorstvedt for the opening goal. Gazza collapsed after trying to form part of the wall, and was carted off to hospital with a cruciate ligament injury that was to keep him out of action for over a year.

Stud Marks

6/10

Gascoigne lay in a hospital bed, aware that he had acted like "a mad bastard" and worried that he screwed up his lucrative move to Lazio. But at least he had Five Bellies for company and his faithful friend, armed with aforementioned airgun, helped him recuperate by sniping at the photographers posted outside the building.

8

Peter McParland
on Ray Wood
Aston Villa v Manchester United
FA Cup final. Wembley. May 1957

Psychologists often refer to the state of cognitive dissonance – a condition describing the uncomfortable tension which results from holding conflicting thoughts in the mind at the same time. It was a predicament first identified by Dr Leon Festinger in 1956, conveniently giving a name to the mental friction referee Frank Coultas was to experience in the aftermath of the following year's FA Cup final. The official confided to one national newspaper reporter that he had been suffering from a migraine for two days after the final, as he wrestled with his conscience over his decision not to send off Peter McParland for an abominable sixth-minute challenge by the Aston Villa left-winger on United goalkeeper Ray Wood. His action, at best negligent, left Wood with a broken cheekbone and consigned to stagger uselessly up and down the touchline for the remainder of the match – no substitutes were allowed in those days – and Jackie Blanchflower, the cultured United centre-half, taking over between the posts. He was helpless to deny Villa's match-winner: the reprieved McParland, who scored twice. The shoulder-charge was perfectly legal, but Wood had already taken a couple of steps to steady himself and was several yards from goal when McParland made his nauseating connection.

Stud Marks

7/10

Matt Busby refused to make the injury an excuse for the 2-1 defeat which deprived his team of the double but United's fans were less forgiving, booing McParland whenever he touched the ball. Wood later suggested, with disarming understatement, that the challenge had been "unnecessary" and it was the Villa man who seemed more incensed, pointing out that he had "got a crack in the face myself". Coultas, meanwhile, was last heard of blabbering to anyone who'd listen that the jeering was "most unfair. I'm sure he didn't mean to hurt him."

9

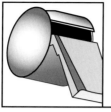

Lee Wilkie on Barry Ferguson and Giovanni van Bronckhorst
Dundee v Rangers
Scottish Premier League, Dens Park, October 1999

You can blame the impetuosity of youth, you can blame bad timing, but by any stretch of the imagination, the challenge that resulted in Lee Wilkie's first sending-off at any level was special. What made it noteworthy was the confusion over whether the 19-year-old defender's lunge that took out Barry Ferguson and Giovanni van Bronckhorst in quick succession was actually two tackles or two parts of the same tackle, linked only by the defender's furious momentum. Whichever, it/they was/were (delete as appropriate) blatantly bestial enough that referee Stuart Dougal had produced a straight red almost before Wilkie's follow-through was complete. The mayhem that ensued, however, was much more mystifying for the official. While Ferguson showed sure signs of distress, lying on the ground beating the turf with his arm, and already wondering whether he'd be fit for Scotland's forthcoming match against Bosnia, van Bronckhorst kicked out in retaliation, prompting players from both sides to square up to each other near the halfway line. James Grady had a yellow card brandished in his direction, and Arthur Numan initially took the rap for van Bronckhorst's reaction when Dougal sent him off, but the referee's assistant stepped in and picked out the true culprit.

Stud Marks

9/10

While van Bronckhorst was left to survey his bruises in the visitors' changing-room bath, Ferguson was strapped up and managed to carry on, as Rangers, 1-0 up at the time, ran out 3-2 winners. Captain Lorenzo Amoruso and Dundee gaffer Jocky Scott differed on the main talking point of the game. While Amoruso raged at Wilkie's tackling, branding him a "stupid hothead", Scott showed Wenger-like myopia, saying: "I thought both challenges were good, especially the first one. He wasn't told why he was sent off and is very upset."

10

Mauricio Taricco on John Moncur: John Moncur on Jose Dominguez

Tottenham Hotspur v West Ham United
The Premiership. White Hart Lane. April 1999

John Moncur was described by one team-mate as the funniest man in football, although it is debatable whether the Covent Garden street performer who found his flame-swallowing act brought to an abrupt end when the West Ham midfielder nipped into a nearby bar, brought out a fire extinguisher and smothered his show with cold foam, would concur. Neither, probably, would Jose Dominguez, Tottenham's lesser-spotted Portuguese winger, after he became the victim of a Moncur challenge so late that it almost ran out of stoppage time. In truth, it had been coming for a while, in a tasty London derby reporters would euphemistically describe as "lively". Taricco's earlier tackle on Moncur was considered "eye-watering" by one writer and "a potential leg-breaker" by Steve Lomas, the Hammers' captain. That engendered an 18-man brawl, and the Argentinian was by all accounts fortunate to escape with a booking. Whether it was a case of mistaken identity or, with time running out, Moncur just wanted to ensure he got in some retribution irrespective of the victim, is not known, but the midfielder made sure he picked on someone his own size, a player of pocket proportions, and flattened him with a horrendous lunge.

Stud Marks

7/10

Moncur was ordered off – he'd already had a yellow – but the foul provoked another group set-to with Stephen Carr allegedly clouting Moncur round the head and David Ginola, hair trailing "elfily" in the breeze, running a good 30 yards to get involved. Spurs manager George Graham accused Moncur of being "childish" but the humorist of Upton Park had the last laugh, as his team left with a 2-1 victory.

11

Defenders visibly winced when Graham Kelly stood up in court to give evidence on behalf of Gary Blissett, and it was not because of the stony-faced FA chief executive's rather humourless visage – think John Prescott with a fatty piece of steak caught in his chops. Of more concern was Kelly's assertion that on any weekend you could expect to see 200 challenges of the type that Blissett had visited upon John Uzzell a few months earlier – a leading elbow into the bridge of the nose. It had left the Torquay centre-back fighting to save his shattered face, not to mention his career, and resulted in the Brentford striker being hauled up before twelve men good and true on a GBH charge. The FA had already knocked back the possibility of a disrepute charge after studying the incident, while Blissett was busy protesting his innocence, despite receiving a red card. Kelly managed to alienate just about everyone with his comments – Torquay, for suggesting that Blissett's challenge was "entirely reasonable", the referees' union for seemingly calling into question one of their members' decisions, and the players' union for intimating that use of the elbow was so prevalent. The only man in football grateful for his intervention was Blissett himself – he was acquitted.

Stud Marks

9/10

*Elbow grease, more like.
Kelly was unrepentant afterwards.
"I was faced with a stark choice," he said.
"To decide whether to avoid upsetting*

referees or to see whether I was free to visit Gary Blissett in jail over Christmas. I chose to tell the truth." He found an unlikely ally in the writer of an editorial in the now-defunct Today *newspaper, who criticised the fact that the incident had gone to court and provided some solace for Blissett himself. "For a man painted as a heartless thug last week," it opined, "Blissett has shown a lot of character. Despite the stigma of facing jail he has so far managed to scored 17 goals for Brentford in the Third Division this season." Uzzell was not impressed and later took a civil action against the striker.*

12 Unused substitute

Blissett may have been the first player to face a criminal charge over a challenge, but the legal route has been one trod increasingly by footballers in the past quarter of a century, especially if their career has been ended prematurely by an over-the-top opponent. John O'Neill, of Norwich, Gordon Watson, of Bradford, Ian Nolan, of Sheffield Wednesday and Jim Brown, of Dunfermline Athletic, are among those who have used the courts or the threat of them to siphon payments out of their assailants – take a bow John Fashanu, Kevin Gray, Justin Edinburgh and John Pelosi. But Matt Holmes, the Charlton Athletic player forced out of the game in 1998 by a Kevin Muscat tackle that left him with a leg injury so severe his surgeons initially contemplated amputation, took his litigation a step further, his lawyers winning dispensation to produce Muscat's previous disciplinary record as evidence against him; eight other tackles by the Australian international were said to have been taken into account before Holmes accepted a £250,000 settlement out of court. It is not known whether one of them was when the Wolves defender's studs perforated Craig Bellamy's knee later the same year, leaving the Norwich City frontman needing nine stitches and a pair of crutches on which to hobble away from Molineux after the game, but Muscat was to get his comeuppance when the teams met at Carrow Road 12 months down the line. The marks of years of combat with spiteful centre halves were apparent all over Iwan Roberts' face, most noticeably his mouth, which had been declared almost a tooth-free zone – but the Canaries' centre forward was prepared to go into battle one more time to avenge his fallen comrade, even though the stamp on Muscat's back did cost him a £2,500 fine and a three-match suspension.

Chapter Two

The worst tantrums

The worst tantrums

Never let it be said that footballers are childish. No, the sight of Gazza massaging his fake tits, belching into the camera or crying when he gets booked in a World Cup semi-final are all, in essence, signs that the game is comfortable with itself and confident in its ability to adapt to an ever-changing world. OK, sometimes players do get a bit upset, but it's often in the heat of the moment and, if not, there are usually compelling reasons. For it's a tough world out there, one in which a team-mate may be earning a few million quid more than you, one in which a fan (what do they know?) may be questioning whether you're worthy of the slab of gold bullion you take out of the club each week, one in which a referee may be harshly judging your tackles on the basis of that video you endorsed, for a few extra loose notes, saluting the art of the crunching challenge from behind. Not that there isn't a place for a bit of good old-fashioned rage in the game. Indeed, it has been known to bring about change of benefit to the sport as a whole: if Aston Villa goalkeeper Bill Dunning hadn't angrily booted the ball out of the stadium when Stoke were given a last-minute penalty in a match in 1892, the FA wouldn't have wised up to the gamesmanship implications of not adding on time to allow a spot-kick to be taken. And let us not just single out the players, for such petulance is not the preserve of them alone; referees and managers have had their moments too, as is revealed in the following selection...

1

Neville Southall
Everton v Leeds United
Division One, Goodison Park, August 1990

You can take the boy out of refuse collection but you can't take the refuse collector out of the boy. Or that, at least, was what a couple of Everton fans were intent on impressing on Neville Southall as he took the pitch for the second match of the season away to Coventry. Greeted not by cheers but by a banner portraying him as "Judas" and pointing out that he was "once a binman, always a binman", the goalkeeper, who numbered hod-carrying among his other previous occupations before he was swept from the streets to become custodian for Bury, might have wondered why the pair, angered by the Welshman's behaviour in the season's opener against Leeds four days earlier, had chosen to focus on this particular element of his past life to register their disapproval; was it snobbish disdain for the working classes, or had they just had a nasty experience with a dustcart in adolescence?

Whichever, it was not surprising their ire had been stoked because, by any standards, Southall's behaviour before the second half of the season's opener at Goodison Park was unusual.

Leaving his team-mates behind in the dressing room, Southall trotted back on to the pitch four minutes early, sat down against a post in the Park Road goalmouth, and adopted the demeanour of a man who looked for all the world as though he'd been injured by a sharp object in your bin liner. Supporters thought they knew what was behind his eccentric display, for the man at the time rated by many as the best goalkeeper in the world had, despite having six years of a lucrative contract still to run, recently put in a second transfer request - only to see it swiftly rejected - and their boos provided evidence of their anger.

Rattle Rating

4/10

A shaky 4/10. Southall had always been a bit of an individual and it was later claimed his behaviour had been born not of petulance, but the desire to hot-foot it from the half-time haranguing he and his defenders were getting from manager Colin Harvey for a hapless 45 minutes that saw them trailing 2-0. Nevertheless, he found his pockets lightened by £3,000 when he was fined a week's wages.

43

2

Ratsimandresy Ratsarazaka

AS Adema v Stade Olympique l'Ermyne

Madagascan League play-offs, Toamasina, October 2002

For a poor nation, the literacy rate in Madagascar is relatively high at 71%, but it is not so much the three r's that have helped put the country on the world stage as the 11 r's – in the 2006 World Cup qualifier against Tunisia, every player's name began with the letter. A statistical oddity for sure, but the nation's real claim to footballing fame comes from the realm of its domestic football, and the ability of the Stade Olympique coach Ratsimandresy Ratsarazaka to attract headlines for reasons other than his initials. When his side lined up opposite AS Adema in the country's league play-offs, Ratsarazaka

was seething with a rage that only a man with ten syllables to his name can muster. For the match was effectively meaningless, Adema having secured the championship the previous weekend after a hotly-disputed refereeing decision had enabled them to draw against Dornoina Savina Astimondrano. Ratsarazaka, whose team had been defending their title, felt wronged and, presuming that a complaint to the country's FA would be treated with the usual disdain of football bureaucrats, decided to show his contempt for the authorities in a uniquely self-destructive way. With his skipper Mamisoa Razafindrakato marshalling things from midfield, the team simply delivered the ball from the centre spot to their own net from each kick-off until the referee, no doubt perplexed but playing it by the letter nonetheless, blew for full time. It left the Adema players bemused – not to mention peeved at being unable to try out the latest free kick routine they'd been working on in training – the fans demanding their money back, and a final score of 149-0.

Rattle Rating

9/10

A reverberating 9/10. Such

is the global village that we now live in, actions in one part of the world can have devastating effects elsewhere on the earth. In this case, the quiet Scottish town of Arbroath, whose football team could see their small place in history – their record 36–0 win over Bon Accord in 1885 – being wiped off the map. John Christison, the club's chairman, was incandescent, arguing that the result from Madagascar should not be ratified by FIFA – though their own record is questionable, as the Bon Accord side were actually an Aberdeen cricket team. Meanwhile, back in the Indian Ocean, Ratsarazaka was paying for the fittest of piques with a three-year suspension.

Bert Trautmann
Manchester City v Charlton Athletic
Division One, Maine Road, November 1954

Trautmann had a hard time being accepted when he first moved into professional football with Manchester City – the German former prisoner-of-war was the subject of protest letters, abusive phone calls and the vitriol of the Jewish community when he was signed from amateurs St Helens – but for someone who had survived a burst appendix and an exploding train in his years on the Russian front, it was nothing he couldn't deal with, and he won over even his fiercest critics with his disarmingly friendly demeanour. All of which would suggest that he really must have been having an off-day – City certainly were as they went down 5-1 – to have started so openly disputing many of the referee's decisions against Charlton. Eventually, after a penalty had been awarded to the Londoners, he was asked for his name and derisively replied: "Stanley Matthews". The referee was not fooled and, fortunate not to have been given his marching orders, Trautmann pushed his luck further when he refused to stand and face Eddie Firmani's spot kick; when he was finally persuaded to take up his position on the line, he stood bolt upright and made no attempt to save the shot.

Rattle Rating

9/10

A judderingly unusual 9/10. The uncharacteristic show of contempt earned Trautmann a two-game suspension – the first games he had missed for City since making his league debut in 1949.

Eddie Green
Farnborough v Purfleet
Isthmian League. Cherrywood Road.
October 1999

Jack Howcroft, a referee in the 1920s, once stopped a match at West Ham to address some rowdy spectators who had questioned one of his decisions. It can be assumed that the negotiations went relatively smoothly, and both sides were happy to at least agree to disagree, because the match continued without any similar stoppages. But for some referees, the continual flak eventually takes its toll and for the sake of their health, they decide to see out the remainder of the season before quietly retiring from the game to which they have given their best years. Sometimes though, their departure can be abrupt. Like that of Eddie Green, the official in this fixture, who, questioned at half-time by Purfleet manager Colin McBride over the booking of Jimmy McFarlane, the Essex side's central defender, suddenly realised he could take no more. A quarter of a century of pent-up fury, humiliation and downright despair at the way the sport was heading was finally liberated as Green quit on the spot, leaving the 374 spectators to wait 25 minutes while a replacement official was located. Tracked down later to his Surrey hideout, Green continued the purification process. "I do not need all the grief I received as I got into the tunnel," he told the *Farnborough News*. "I do my best, but if that's not good enough, then that's it. The players are cheats nowadays and I'm no longer prepared to take it. I've been abused for 25 years and I've had enough."

Rattle Rating

7/10

A rumbling 7/10.

Would have had greater repercussions if someone had done it in the Premiership, but Green's stand was at least proof that without referees there can be no game. McBride, though, was puzzled: "I know it's unusual," the away team's boss said, "but I didn't swear or have a go at him, honest."

Keith Weller
Leicester City v Ipswich Town
Division One. Filbert Street. December 1974

I t was the Friday before Christmas, but Keith Weller was not in the party mood. The Leicester City midfielder had put in a transfer request, had had it turned down and been stripped of the captaincy for his troubles. When the crowd began to get on his back after the club, already struggling against relegation, fell behind to Ipswich, it was the final straw – the former Tottenham, Millwall and Chelsea player booted the ball into the stands in his frustration before, on the half-time whistle, running down the tunnel, jumping into the dressing-room bath and refusing to come out, even when manager Jimmy

Bloomfield, who first tried to bribe him by offering him later sole use of the team bubble bath, warned him of the consequences. Those consequences were decided the following Monday when the board met to discuss the incident, though it has to be said that, on the surface, they didn't sound too severe: Weller was forced to train on his own for a week and missed the Boxing Day defeat by Queens Park Rangers, their seventh in eight games.

Rattle Rating
5/10

A jangling 5/10. Weller made all the right noises of contrition, apologising profusely to the supporters for his behaviour, and some months later withdrawing his transfer request, but there was an upside to his festive folly: "I got to spend more time with my family", he told one newspaper, "and I didn't have to watch what I ate."

6

Eric Cantona
Crystal Palace v Manchester United
The Premiership. Selhurst Park.
January 1995

As a quote, Eric Cantona's observation that "criticism is like a toilet and it means nothing to me", was not only not quite in the same league as his poetic utterances on seagulls and trawlers, but also not strictly accurate. Ask Michel Bernardet and Jean-Claud Lemoult, two team-mates at Montpellier, how little criticism meant to him, and they will show you the indentations the enfant terrible left on their skulls with repeated use of his boot after they questioned his commitment following a defeat at Lille. Or ask Matthew Simmons, who transformed himself from unknown Crystal Palace supporter to national hate figure in little more than the time that it took him to race down the steps of the Main Stand at Selhurst Park and offer his opinion of the player's mother to a departing Cantona, sent off for kicking out at Richard Shaw. The prickly Frenchman's response to Simmons' baiting – a two-footed lunge across the advertising hoardings into the supporter's midriff that bore the hallmarks of a man who had watched too many Bruce Lee videos – was to become an iconic image of the 1990s.

Rattle Rating

11/10

A clattering 11/10. Cantona eventually came up if not smelling of roses, at least wearing the fragrance of fresh cash. He may have been one of the few players in history to have attacked a fan, causing some outrage initially, but when Simmons was revealed to have once roughed up a petrol station attendant with a spanner and then, at his own court hearing for threatening behaviour, leapt from the witness box to launch a Cantona-like assault on the prosecuting counsel – he grabbed him by the throat and pulled his tie off before being restrained by six police officers – the Frenchman's sense of self-righteousness was reinforced and advertisers queued up to get him to endorse their products. His prison sentence was reduced on appeal to 120 hours' community service, but the FA banned him until the next September.

7

In The Case of the Boot and the Eyebrow, even the most slothful sleuth in the journalistic pack was not required to put in too much detective work to discover the guilty party: the answer was written all over David Beckham's face, or, more specifically, his forehead. When he emerged from the Old Trafford dressing-room 25 minutes before the rest of the team in patched-up state after being forced to take the rap for Arsenal's second goal in his team's 2-0 defeat – and a rogue boot in the skull from his manager – reporting instincts were immediately aroused, and the facts, or versions of them, were in the public domain before Sir Alex Ferguson had had time to repeat his well-worn mantra of what happens in the dressing room stays in the dressing room. But if Beckham was stitched up, it was as nothing compared to his boss, whose apology to the England captain before he swept away from the ground was not, apparently, enough for a man who later admitted that he had wanted Ferguson to go public with his regret. Going public was not something Beckham had too much difficulty with and while he didn't come straight out and give an unabridged account of what had happened, journalists knew when he went shopping in Manchester two days later with his hair held clear of his forehead by an Alice band, it was not just another fashion statement, and it kept the speculation about the breakdown in the pair's relationship on the boil for months to come.

Rattle Rating

10/10

A rumbling great 10/10.
Although Ferguson went out of his way to praise Beckham's contribution after his next game, against Juventus in the Champions League, the damage was done and a parting of the ways became inevitable. The player put out a statement saying that the boot incident was an accident – and the Scotsman's own account suggested he could not have achieved similar accuracy if he'd tried it a million times – but Beckham teasingly left the door open for a different interpretation when he recounted the incident in his autobiography, saying Ferguson had swung his foot at the boot on the dressing room floor and he wasn't sure whether it was "at me, or at the wall".

8

Billy Cook
Middlesbrough v Oldham Athletic
Division One. Ayresome Park. April 1915

Oldham full back Billy Cook was seen as something of a gentleman among players – he played cricket for Lancashire, for goodness sake – but he caused a bit of a stir with his actions in this wartime match that, if reports are to be believed, was akin to a series of bayonet charges into No Man's Land. "Men ran riot, losing their heads and hurling themselves into each other in a manner that boded ill for the combatants," read one despatch from Ayresome Park. "I feared the climax would be the maiming of one". Which is why when, after referee H Smith had ignored a nailed-on handball on the line by the home side and allowed them a goal the visitors were sure was offside, as well as turning a blind eye to some of the more malevolent challenges, Cook was astounded to find himself pointed to the dressing room for a minor trip on England amateur Henry Carr. It was, in the veteran defender's view, a crass decision and he reacted to it by simply refusing to budge – a pointless move as it turned out, because Smith responded by abandoning the match, with half an hour still to go.

Rattle Rating
6/10

An echoing 6/10. If Cook thought Oldham, challenging for the title at the time, would benefit from his stance, he quickly had his illusions shattered: a Football League commission a week later ordered the 4–1 scoreline in favour of Middlesbrough to stand, while Cook was suspended for a year. And Oldham lost out on the championship to Everton by one point which, conceivably, they could have hauled back if they'd finished the match.

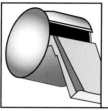

9

The Palmeiras team
Corinthians v Palmeiras
Brazilian Championship. Parque São Jorge.
July 1999

Brazilians may have put a more skilful spin on the British game – even Ronaldo's wife once led the world in keepy-uppies (55,187 touches if you've mislaid your *Guinness Book of Records*), but all this flair and invention and football for its own sake was not always appreciated, not even by their fellow countrymen. As Edilson, the Corinthians star, found when, having helped his team to build a 3-0 lead in the Paulista finals, he decided to indulge in a little showboating. A touch of juggling with the ball on your own is innocent enough, you might think, and all part of the rich palate of football in this neck of the woods, but it was too much for the Palmeiras players, whose attempts to bring a halt to his party tricks sparked a brawl and a riot by fans.

Rattle Rating
6/10

A ringing 6/10. Top example of the team tantrum. Edilson was later dropped from the national squad by coach Vanderlei Luxemburgo, who echoed the thoughts of the Palmeiras side that day when he explained why. "I just don't like his attitude," he said.

10

Leo Roget
Southend v Barnet
Division Three. Roots Hall.
December 1999

Flourishing football clubs often talk of the importance of their back-room staff: the reserve team coaches, the medical team, the scouting team and, almost as often these days, the psychologists and counsellors, all of whom can play their part in giving their side the edge in motivation and morale. But there is one other influence behind the scenes whose significance has grown: the ghetto-blaster. Enough to frighten an elderly kit-man into emptying the club Persil on the laundry floor, it usually booms out its bombastic message of arrogance and intimidation in the build-up to kick-off, but it has also been used, more unsportingly, at the end of matches to trumpet the message of supremacy to the opponents across the corridor – as happened when Barnet celebrated their 3-1 triumph at Southend. The North Londoners pumped up the volume to a point where an enraged Leo Roget, the Southend defender, could stand it no more. Stomping over to the other dressing-room, he made a scathing comment on Barnet's musical preferences by ripping out the plug and smashing the machine repeatedly against the floor.

Rattle Rating
9/10

A screeching 9/10. Forced to face the music, Roget's actions cost him a week's wages, but my, it must have felt good.

11

Ian Wright
West Ham United v Leeds United
The Premiership. Upton Park. May 1999

I t was widely implied by participants and the media that Rob Harris, as the referee who sent off three West Ham players in this match, had lost the plot. But if that was true, Ian Wright, the first of those to receive the red card, could probably be considered to have mislaid the characters and the first three chapters, as his dismissal in the 16th minute sparked a narrative that his team-mates found hard to believe when they first read about it in the next day's papers. Storming into the tunnel, he failed to follow the usual storyline, which would have taken him to the home dressing-room and under a cool shower, where he could reflect more soberly on the events that had led to his premature departure. Instead, he seemed to be making it up as he went along, first practically tearing the door of the referee's room off its hinges before dumping a television and the official's clothing into the bath. The forward didn't even stay around for the fallout: he stomped to his car still in his shirt, shorts and boots and drove straight home.

Rattle Rating

9/10

A resonating 9/10, it was a case of worst tantrum, best apology, as Wright sought to stave off FA retribution through the columns of The Sun. "I was furious at being sent off for only the second time in my career," he sobbed unconvincingly. "I was disappointed at letting down my manager, my team-mates and the West Ham fans by not being on the pitch to help win the game and get us into Europe. But most of all, I was disappointed in myself. I was so upset that I behaved in an unacceptable manner. I hope and pray to God that I can be forgiven for this stupid and reckless act by the match officials, the club, the fans and the authorities." No chance, mate! He was banned for three matches and given a £17,500 fine.

12 Unused substitute

It was four days after he had refused to shake hands with Jesse Owens, the black American who had won the 100 metres, and Adolf Hitler was trying to decide which sport in the 1936 Berlin Olympics to next grace with his presence. Rowing and polo were options, and sounded nice. Then someone in his entourage of evil suggested football. Bad career move. The Fuhrer had never seen a match, and consented to the idea, trooping down to the Poststadion with Goebbels, Goering and Hess in anticipation of watching Otto Nerz's German team lay waste to the Norwegians. Germany had beaten Luxembourg 9-0 in the first match of the tournament and had not lost to Norway in eight previous internationals, so when the Scandinavians took the lead after six minutes it was enough to have Goebbels quaking in his jackboots. As the Germans lay siege to the Norwegian goal, he noted with some concern in his diary that "the Fuhrer is very agitated" – and the Fuhrer became even more disturbed when, with only a few minutes remaining, a breakaway brought the underdogs a second goal, effectively eliminating the hosts from the tournament. This was unpredictable – and the Nazis didn't do unpredictable. With Goebbels slipping ever lower in his seat, Hitler jumped to his feet, possibly stamped one of them on the hard concrete floor of the main stand, and stormed out of the stadium.

Chapter Three

The worst brawls, tunnel incidents and training-ground bust-ups

Worst brawls, tunnel incidents

Having admitted defeat in the fight against real crime, the Crown Prosecution Service started to mull over the possibility of bringing brawling footballers to justice. The move was instigated after a supporter at the match in which team-mates Kieron Dyer and Lee Bowyer came to blows (of which, more later) "raised concerns" about their behaviour. It would, perhaps, have been of more benefit to the future of English football if said spectator had raised concerns about their abilities with the ball at their feet. For, if the CPS's action was aimed at ensuring players

& training-ground bust-ups

create a good impression on the young, it was doomed to failure – the average teenager will encounter more vicious and senseless violence on a daily basis on his video game console and mobile phone. Besides, violence is at the heart of the entertainment business and has been for centuries – why else would the Royal Shakespeare Company's marketing initiative of 1997 have played up the savagery of its production of Henry V with adverts in the sports pages proclaiming: "In 1415, away games were a matter of life and death." No, the CPS should focus their energies on more damaging felonies and allow the rest of us to appreciate those captivating, although still relatively rare, moments when competitive spirit and ego combine to produce something shocking, yes, ugly, undoubtedly, but strangely fascinating nonetheless.

1

Manchester United
v Arsenal

The Premiership, Old Trafford, October 2004

Girly stuff, but given far too much status by hype. If the sight of Sir Alex Ferguson batting away an Ashley Cole-propelled slice of Four Seasons from the bridge of his purple nose was as bad as the acres of column inches used to recount it suggested, planet football really was on collision course with a wayward asteroid. It wasn't, and Fergie himself was initially keen to downplay the incident that erupted backstage in the aftermath of a match that produced Arsenal's first defeat for 50 matches and started a run that ultimately cost them their Premiership title. But journalists who had spent the previous few weeks building the match up as "the game of the decade" were not going to be denied their pound of outrage, and though both boardrooms sought to call a truce, the media managed to keep it simmering until the teams met again and the managers complied with the agenda by launching a tit-for-tat verbal skirmish. Ferguson embarked on a tirade condemning Arséne Wenger for never apologising, accused him of challenging him to a fight in the Old Trafford corridors and branded the Gunners "the worst losers of all time".

Pizza Rating
3/10

Storm in a very deep pan. In the run-up to the February game, sports minister Richard Caborn urged the managers to "cool it" while the officer in charge of policing the match also called on them to halt their war of words for fear of the bad feeling spilling over into the stands. In the event, Ferguson left Highbury licking his lips over nothing more tasty than United's 4-2 victory.

2

Brian Laws v Ivano Bonetti
Luton Town v Grimsby Town
Division One. Kenilworth Road. February 1996

The Italian male's love of food is legendary, his ability to immerse himself in gastronomic revelry often taking precedence over his affections for his wife, his children, and sometimes, even, his football team. Thus when Ivano Bonetti came off the pitch after Grimsby had thrown away a lead to let Luton beat them 3-2 on a cold midweek night at Kenilworth Road, he shrugged his shoulders in the continental manner – and hared up the tunnel to be first in the queue for the large tray of chicken wings that had been left by their hosts on a table in the middle of the dressing room. Unfortunately, Brian Laws, his manager, had beaten him to it and when he saw Bonetti race in and reach unhesitatingly for the edibles rather than taking time to inwardly digest the loss of another three points, he exploded as if he had himself consumed an ovenful of the greasy fare, flattening the former Juventus winger with a blow that fractured his cheekbone and condemned him to a two-hour operation and several days of hospital cuisine.

Pizza Rating

8/10

Off the menu. Details of

the confrontation were slow to seep out, with Laws at first prepared to admit only that "a regrettable incident did take place" and, although the pair tried to make their peace with a handshake before the match at West Ham 11 days later, Laws was fined by his club and slapped with an FA charge to boot. If Laws thought things could only get better, he was a few herbs short of the complete calzone; in November, Bonetti won a civil lawsuit against him and Grimsby suggested he might like to find alternative employment.

3

Francis Lee v Norman Hunter
Derby County v Leeds United
Division One. the Baseball Ground.
November 1975

Francis Lee, barrel-chested and only 5'7", had a low centre of gravity, meaning that he went to ground easily. Or he dived a lot. In apparent revenge for a penalty Lee had won following an uncharacteristically innocuous challenge by Hunter, hostilities re-erupted early in the second half. Lee shot, Hunter's tackle was later than a Virgin train, and all hell broke loose. Referee Derek Nippard thought he'd nipped it in the bud by sending both off – at the time, Lee merely had a cut lip that would require stitches – but trouble flared again en route to the cold showers, this time spurred by a verbal disagreement over whose fault it was. Team-mates dived in again, mainly to drag them off each other, although Billy Bremner, an unlikely peacemaker, was spotted trying to get a dig in. Lee later challenged

Hunter, in an interview with his local paper, to a "fight on any cobbled street he cares to choose" – with the £40,000 Hunter received from his testimonial as the prize fund. Not surprisingly the 32-year-old Hunter, in his last few months with the club, didn't want to risk his nest-egg. "I don't mind mixing it with him on the field," he said, "but off the pitch is another matter."

Pizza Rating

7/10

Kitchen closed. Lee might

have thought he had had the last word when Roger Davies's scorching drive three minutes from the end of one of the season's best games gave Derby a 3-2 victory, but the former Manchester City man ended up on the receiving end of a guilty verdict after being charged with bringing the game into disrepute, while Hunter got off. More harmful in the short term, though, was the immediate one-match ban that meant he missed his side's return leg against Real Madrid in the European Cup: leading 4-1 from the first match, Derby slumped to a 5-1 reverse without him.

4 Caesar Romero and Giorgio Chinaglia
Chicago Sting v New York Cosmos
North American Soccer League.
Chicago Bowl. July 1982

When the Americans got round to setting up their first professional football league, the NASL, in the late seventies, they weren't content to make do with the identifying marks that had served footballing powers in Europe well for almost a century. While a Bayern was sufficient for the likes of a metropolis of Munich's size, a United and a City acceptable to cover Manchester, and the odd Sporting or Atletico adequate for the largest conurbations in the Latin nations, Stateside found it necessary to invent ever more extraordinary appellations to show just how fantastically awesome was their competition: if

Toronto Blizzard had to call on a weather phenomenon to add some gloss to their image, San Jose Earthquake went one better by evoking a natural disaster; if Los Angeles Aztecs brought to mind a revered ancient civilisation, New York ensured they had the last word by anointing themselves the Cosmos. With such immodesty, it was fitting that the outfit from the Big Apple should be able to attract a galaxy of stars to adorn their colours, such as the Paraguayan boy-wonder Romero and the slightly fading Italian Chinaglia. This match against the Chicago Sting had been hard fought, but there was some even harder fighting to come as the teams left the pitch.

When, without warning, Romero fell to the ground, clutching his face, it quickly became apparent that, because Chicago were trooping off at another corner of the ground, he must have been laid out by one of his team-mates. When Romero jumped up , raced towards Chinaglia, shouting "I'll kill him, I'll kill him", it was evident that that the New York No 9 was the team-mate responsible. Only the swift intervention of the referee and other team-mates prevented further blows being exchanged, but there was only a brief respite, the fighting recommencing once the pair reached the dressing-room and the warring parties having to be separated again, Romero ending up having to take his shower in the referee's changing-room.

Pizza Rating

6/10

Super-size Americana with all the extra toppings: this was the States after all. Chinaglia, a former Italy international, was not a man used to accepting second billing – he had been known to fight his own team-mates for the ball – and it soon emerged that his temper had been stirred because Romero had failed to pass to him during the match. At least their disagreement was not a lasting one: later that night the pair were spotted sharing a couple of beers at a downtown hotel.

John Fashanu
v Lawrie Sanchez
Wimbledon training ground. July 1993

John Fashanu liked to think of himself as a man of many dimensions: if he wasn't presenting sports programmes of a gladiatorial nature on television, he was probably negotiating another perfectly legitimate business deal in Nigeria, or fine-tuning his latest move in the martial art of Sam Tu Dang.

Occasionally, he would even turn up for a spot of training, although not usually until Friday and then he preferred to pop in for a bit of treatment from the team masseur before, if he was feeling really energetic, joining in a little light five-a-side. It was behaviour tolerated by a succession of Wimbledon managers as long as they could be sure that he would do the business on a Saturday afternoon, but behaviour that left one of his team-mates in this remarkably close-knit club a seething mass of resentment. The former Barnardo's Boy hardly rose in Lawrie Sanchez's estimation when he charged a night of drinking in the hotel bar on one away trip to the midfielder's bill. The confrontation that had been seven years in the making was coming nicely to the boil and finally erupted at a pre-season training session near the end of July 1993. While the two tramped off into a corner of the training ground to see if there was any way in which they could reconcile their differences, the coaching staff were alerted, although no one intervened. Years in the future, dressing-rooms would still recall what was seen in the ensuing minutes – a period that Sanchez was later to refer to as High Noon. It was truly no contest, as Fashanu unfurled his black belt and Sanchez responded with his degree in business management. Time and again the midfielder with the knack for scoring crucial goals was knocked to the floor, but time and again he got back up to take more

punishment, until the pair had battled to a standstill.

Pizza Rating

9/10

Thick crust with chilli and jalapeno pepper – Sanchez was nicknamed 'The Mexican' after all. One Wimbledon team-mate claimed it was more bloody than a spaghetti western, "the most brutal thing I had ever seen, horrible to watch, but it earned Sanchez a lot of respect. No-one had dared to defy Fashanu in such a way before."

6

Naples v Burnley
Fairs Cup, St Paolo Stadium, February 1967

Having incurred the wrath of the Zurich-based Fairs Cup committee for the way they'd dished out the rough stuff during their 3-0 first-leg defeat, Napoli president Giocchine Lauro promised journalists that his team would show, in the return in Italy, "what good sportsmen we are". Just a few minutes were left when Napoli, having made no inroads into Burnley's advantage, broke the promise. Omar Sivori viciously elbowed Dave Merrington in the stomach before heading for Les Latcham. The final whistle went; Alberto Orlando spat in the face of the visiting keeper Harry Thompson when the custodian tried to shake hands. It was Thompson's understudy Adam Blacklaw who, trying to prevent violence between the two, found himself pinned down and being used for volleying practice by a dozen stadium staff. Managing to break free only after sending one of the Italian stewards careering head-first down the stone steps leading to the tunnel, Blacklaw scarpered for the relative safety of the dressing-room, where a bizarre tug-of-war ensued, with Italian police trying to haul Blacklaw into the corridor while his team-mates tried to heave him back in. When one of the cops drew back his overcoat to reveal a revolver, Blacklaw's team-mates knew when they were beaten and retreated to leave him to his fate.

Pizza Rating
9/10
Napoletena, naturally.
Creation of the modern pizza – it was historically a Greek food – is credited to Rafaele Esposito, a Naples baker, but he was not required to provide a sample of his expertise as Burnley forewent the post-match meal and their coach was escorted hastily out of the city by an armoured lorry, nine jeep-loads of militia and several police outriders. Poor Blacklaw, later released with an apology and a very sore head, had to find his own way to the airport.

7

Barnsley v
Bolton Wanderers

FA Cup third round. Oakwell. January 1998

True brawls have their own momentum, a domino effect in which every action produces a reaction, in which one push becomes two shoves becomes three punches becomes seven potatoes more. And they need only the tiniest of sparks to get going. So when Bolton defender Neil Cox went to retrieve a ball that had gone out of play in front of the home team's dugout, it only needed a moment of hesitation from the Barnsley bench in returning it for a fair old scrap to ensue. Cox pushed one of the Yorkshire side's backroom staff, and Barnsley's Eric Winstanley shoved Cox in the back. Within a barely discernible instant, players, substitutes, managers, coaches, and police were involved in a seething mass of mayhem comprising several individual exchanges, the most sinister of which was the right hook from one steward who, unable to resist the unexpected opportunity for a spot of savagery, left Jamie Pollock a staggering shambles.

Pizza Rating

4/10

Small helping of bruschetta. Almost as soon as it had started, it was over – too quickly, seemingly, for it to have lodged on referee David Elleray's hard drive. "I saw little of what was happening," he said. *"Nothing untoward happened. It was a typical English cup-tie. I enjoyed it."*

8

Trevor Christie
v Dale Jasper
Mansfield Town v Crewe Alexandra
Division Four. Field Mill. April 1990

There wasn't much to play for in this end-of-season encounter, and you'd normally expect players' minds to be straying towards the fortnight in Magaluf and avoiding nasty tackles. Not, however, Crewe's Dale Jasper, or Mansfield's Trevor Christie. With just a minute to go until half-time, Christie took a quick throw-in to Mark Kearney, only to see Jasper fly in from behind with a crunching, and quite illegal, tackle. Kearney reacted badly, and Jasper added another kick while he was spreadeagled on the ground. It was as clear-cut a sending-off offence as you could wish to witness, but before the referee had had a chance to reach into his pocket, Christie had taken the law into his own hands and run over and flattened Jasper with a textbook left hook. The Mansfield striker was obviously perturbed to see his opponent beat the count, and when the official dismissed both in quick succession, Christie resolved to finish off the job: catching up with Jasper as he reached the tunnel, he southpawed him again and, for good measure, started to bang his head against the wall.

Pizza Rating
6/10

Vegetariana, with extra wild rocket. Christie was apprehended by the police and left facing a possible assault charge, while Jasper needed stitches in a head wound.

9

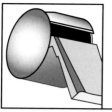

Aranxta v Kevin Lamey
Toros Neza v Jamaica
Friendly. Toluca. Mexico. March 1997

I t only takes a second to score a goal and only a few moments for a small flare-up, but, for the brawl to end all brawls, you need to set aside, say, five or ten minutes, time enough indeed for the warring parties to slip away and arm themselves with their weapon of choice – a chair leg, for example, a large piece of wood, perhaps, or, this being Mexico, a discarded bottle of Corona – and rejoin battle. A late tackle by Stephen Malcolm led to him brawling with his victim, Aranxta, and all 22 players and both benches waded into the maelstrom. Malcolm was kicked and punched, and after his team-mates had gone to his aid, the Mexicans, strengthened by about 200 spectators, advanced on their outnumbered opponents, who were forced to resort to the desperate, defensive measures outlined above. Well, not entirely defensive. The abiding image to emerge, from the tangle of arms, legs and dust kicked up in the bedlam, was the photograph wired to Jamaica's main daily paper, *The Gleaner*, which showed Kevin Lamey, the Jamaica forward, arriving as if fired from a giant high-velocity rifle out of picture on the right, fully horizontal, his studs about to make searing contact with an opponent's kidneys.

Pizza Rating

1o/1o

The game, not surprisingly, was abandoned and the Jamaicans *retreated to their hotel to lick their wounds, among them a swollen face for Rene Simoes, the director of football, and a broken wrist for Onandi Lowe. The staff at their accommodation consoled them with the information that Toros Neza were renowned for such behaviour. Less pacifying was the treatment handed out by FIFA, who fined them 50,000 Swiss francs and warned them they faced World Cup expulsion, while inflicting penalties of just SwF10,000 on Toros Neza and SwF25,000 on the Mexican FA for failing to maintain order.*

10

Lee Bowyer v Kieron Dyer
Newcastle United v Aston Villa
The Premiership. St James's Park. April 2005

L ondon born and bred, Lee Bowyer had found it hard settling in the north, first at Leeds and later at Newcastle. It didn't help that the midfielder, whose misdemeanours had found him embroiled in police investigations in the capital and also while at Elland Road, was not a well-liked individual – in fact, as Tony Cascarino was to mention in a newspaper column: "Everyone I talk to thinks he's a toerag." And when a week that started with his long-term girlfriend reportedly walking out on him ended with a midfield colleague refusing to pass to him from a free-kick during a humiliating home defeat, he countered with the only reasonable response available to him: a headbutt and a punch administered to the perpetrator, Kieron Dyer. Dyer was not one to run away from a confrontation – although he must have fancied scarpering after pranging his high-performance car on the Tyne Bridge for the umpteenth time – and retaliated in kind, an action that led to the duo brawling in front of their own fans and resulted in the pair, shirts hanging by a thread, becoming the first team-mates to be sent off for fighting each other in England since Mike Flanagan and Derek Hales, of Charlton Athletic, in 1979.

Pizza Rating
2/10
Meat feast with chilli on

the top, it was no way for Newcastle to celebrate Alan Shearer signing on for an extra year. Chairman Freddy Shepherd exonerated Dyer of blame, fined Bowyer enough to pay off a Third World country's debt – six weeks' wages – and reinvested it in the club's academy, while the rest of the country revelled in the latest descent of Graeme Souness's men into the theatre of the absurd. That reached its nadir when the warring parties were paraded before the press to show there were no hard feelings, wearing smiles as genuine as the staged shake of hands.

Chesterfield v Plymouth

With less than a minute remaining in his first game back following a holiday in Tenerife, referee Richard Poulain had reason to believe that, despite having to dismiss Plymouth's Ronnie Mauge near the end of the first half for a thundering challenge on Chris Beaumont, the break had refreshed him and his return to action had gone well. Then Chesterfield's Darren Carr thundered into Bruce Grobbelaar, and up to 18 players became embroiled in the sensational scrap that followed, with two getting caught in the Plymouth net as they slugged it out and two more going at each other just outside the 18-yard box. Stewards, supporters and members of the Plymouth bench spilled on to the pitch, adding to the confused jumble of bodies; Poulain must have wished he was safely back in the Canaries scouring the pool area for a free sunbed rather than having to identify the chief culprits of a free-for-all. Nevertheless, he was confident he had fingered the right men when, after the dust settled, he produced red cards for Carr, team-mate Kevin Davies and Plymouth pair Richard Logan and Tony James, becoming the first official in English league football to dismiss five players in one game.

Pizza Rating

8/10

Managers' special. John Duncan, who had led his Chesterfield side to the quarter-finals of the FA Cup, pointed in mitigation to his team's disciplinary record. "We'd had only one player sent off all season and that was revoked on appeal," he said, while Mick Jones, caretaker boss of Plymouth, admitted to a flawed motivational approach against a club that had enjoyed a giantkilling cup success over Bolton the week before. "It's just possible I may have pumped up my players a little too much," he confessed.

12

Unused substitute

When Cyril the Swan, Swansea's controversial mascot, joined in the players' celebrations after Swansea had scored against Millwall in an FA Cup tie, he was hauled in front of the beak, in the form of the Welsh FA, on a disrepute charge. Although that outpouring of joy was understandable, if misguided, the reaction of Marvin the Moose, the Cambridge United mascot, to a poor refereeing decision, was less defensible, and his vigorous and repetitive hoof gesture, intimating to the crowd the favourite solo off-pitch pastime of the official, earned the dressed-up one a serious dressing-down. And when

Freddy the Fox, the mascot visiting Rochdale from Halifax in September 1999, cocked his leg against the posts in front of the home supporters and issued them with a thumbs down, it showed that simply being fitted into a fleecy representation of a furry creature does not necessarily shear a man of his animal instincts. It was an act that raised the synthetic hackles of Desmond the Dragon, the home side's costumed character, and he unleashed a flurry of punches on his opponent. Believing that a fight between dragon and fox was not a fair contest, the local police dragged Desmond, still breathing fire, off to the local nick.

Chapter Four

The

worst

injuries

The Worst Injuries

If, as Benjamin Franklin said, there are two things in life you can't avoid – death and taxes – it is equally fair to say that the footballer can add another inevitability to that surprisingly short list: injury. At the very least they are an inconvenience, as the Encyclopaedia of British Football readily acknowledges. But should we be at risk of getting overly dramatic, this informative tome on the sport is quick to point out that the majority of these – two-thirds, it estimates – are "minor" in nature, what, in modern-day parlance, might be termed slight knocks. Further comfort for the player comes from the calculation that another quarter – the hamstring pull might fall into this category – are only "moderate in severity". But the remainder, a seemingly measly nine per cent for those of you counting, are the biggies, ones which at the very least can be expected to be accompanied by a stretcher, a posse of St John's Ambulance types and the adjective "career-threatening".

Obviously, it is the last of these three classifications that we are most concerned with here, although, as the following examples show, there is more to the worst injuries than can be discerned from the physical scars alone.

1

Jim McNichol
Torquay United v Crewe Alexandra
Division Four. Plainmoor. May 1987

It is as well for Torquay that dangerous dogs legislation was not introduced in Britain until 1991; had it been on the statutes four years earlier, the modern history of lower-league football could have been altered irrevocably. For while Jim McNichol would have been hard-pushed at the time to appreciate the moment, on the final day of the season, when an Alsatian escaped from its police handler, ran on to the pitch and sank its teeth into his right leg, he, and his team, were later to have reason to be indebted to the dog. Indeed, far from being consigned to a grisly fate in the incinerator at the local vet for being unmuzzled, the animal was rewarded for his intervention – which ultimately condemned Lincoln City – with the biggest steak in the South West, courtesy of a thoroughly appreciative Torquay chairman. At the start of play, the Devon club were one of three teams – Lincoln and Burnley were the others – vulnerable to becoming the first to lose their league status by relegation rather than on a failed re-election attempt. Torquay looked to be in most trouble at half-time, having fallen 2-0 behind, but McNichol scored to put them back in with an outside chance before, in the dying minutes, the home team found providence at the end of a paw: in the last seconds of injury time added for the treatment of McNichol's wound, Paul Dobson sniffed out some space and pounced to snaffle an equaliser.

Pain Threshold

6/10

Hangdog expressions all round for Lincoln, whose own game had ended in defeat at Swansea. Their players were left to gather round a transistor radio to listen to events unfold at Torquay and Turf Moor, where Burnley's match against Orient had also been delayed, in this case by the size of the crowd. When Burnley triumphed, they were left counting on Crewe to see out time at Plainmoor, but Dobson's goal with just seconds to go sent them to the bottom of the league for the first time in the season and facing at least a year of Conference football.

2

Bryn Jones and Ray Jones
Chester v Aldershot
Fourth Division, Sealand Road, January 1966

Scientists have in recent years begun to identify some sort of order in the universe, a creative, if not always benevolent, hand at work. Sometimes, a similar kind of symmetry can be distinguished amid the chaos of football existence. That the two Chester full-backs were both Joneses, Bryn on the right and Ray on the left, might be considered coincidence enough in normal circumstances, although this was the Welsh borders – there were actually four with the surname on the pitch, striker Les completing the Chester triumvirate and David in goal for Aldershot. But it didn't end there: before the afternoon was out, the pair would be lining up together in the A&E department of the local infirmary with a broken left leg apiece. Bryn was first into the ambulance after mistiming a 21st-minute tackle on Aldershot forward Derek Norman, and the visitors added insult to injury by scoring the game's opening goal while he was still writhing in agony on the ground; a few minutes after a different kind of break – the one for half-time – and with the scores level at 2-2, Ray kept up with his namesake, again after a poorly-executed tackle.

Pain Threshold
7/10

High. Ten-man Chester were not to be undone by the untimely fluke of fate and it was Aldershot who began to look disjointed, Mark Metcalf grabbing the winner for the home side late on. But, without their two full-backs for the remainder of the season, their promotion challenge was left more fragmented than a fractured tibia.

Gary Mabbutt
Tottenham Hotspur v Wimbledon
The Premiership. White Hart Lane. November 1993

A couple of weeks after his rumbustious Wimbledon team had grappled their way to another point at White Hart Lane in the top flight's ultimate clash of footballing cultures, Joe Kinnear came out with a comment that left those who heard it uncertain as to whether he was indulging a very black sense of humour or was just callously insensitive. "We enjoy going to the big clubs and putting their faces out of joint," the Irishman said, apparently impervious to the fact that only a fortnight earlier John Fashanu had left the imprint of a wayward forearm deeply imbedded on Gary Mabbutt's visage in a challenge which the Tottenham skipper's mum, Avis, memorably described as "playing football without due care and attention". But while Mabbutt, whose face had taken on a lopsided bearing, was having metal pins inserted into a mashed cheekbone, and surgeons operating on his broken eye socket had to wake him every half-an-hour to ensure he could still see, Fashanu was busy trying to repair his own image, signing up as a roving ambassador for Unicef. Fashanu got an early Christmas present on December 24, avoiding a misconduct charge when an FA Commission was unable to conclude from repeated viewings of the match video that there was deliberate intent on the striker's part.

Pain Threshold
6/10

Ossie Ardiles, the Spurs manager, was incensed, mistakenly accusing the referee, Keith Hackett, of having changed his story, while Wimbledon counterpunched with the accusation that Spurs were making a "crude attempt" to divert attention from financial irregularities at the club. Fears that Mabbutt would never play again proved unfounded and he returned, in full facial mask, later in the season. In the summer, after signing a new contract, he dropped plans to take legal action against Fashanu.

Eddie Mason

Hull City v Lincoln City

Division Two. Anlaby Road. December 1919

Eddie 'Tich' Mason, as his nickname would suggest, could be described as of no more than diminutive build, but his little legs would propel him at a surprisingly quick rate along the right wing, as well as the 100 metres track, where he was a British Services champion. And it was in the service of his country that his fast-twitch muscle fibres proved particularly useful, his ability to rapidly relocate himself in the First World War trenches whenever serious enemy fire was incoming, not to mention a healthy dose of good fortune, enabling him to return to Hull, once hostilities ceased, with all his limbs intact. Yet, all that mobility was to count for nothing when, at the age of 25, he was brought in to make his first appearance for his home-town club: just ten minutes into his debut, a man who had survived the battlefields of Ypres and Marne had become the victim of enemy action. Chasing a ball towards the right corner flag at the Lincoln end, his progress was prematurely terminated by an unidentified defender. Transported to the dressing-room, it became clear that he could not be patched up and sent out again to resume combat.

Pain Threshold

6/10

A serious fracture to the right leg was subsequently diagnosed and a distraught local press was not slow to point out the irony of the injury. In a newspaper interview, Mason, who only weeks earlier had relinquished his amateur status as a runner to turn professional, was upbeat: "I was unlucky to be hurt last week," he said. "But I hope to get a further chance." He did, but not for a while and not for long – returning for two matches ten months later, he was not his speedy self of old and was offloaded to Rotherham, where he never got a game.

5

Bobby Blackwood.
QPR v Colchester United
League Cup 1st round. Loftus Road. August 1966

and Colchester United v QPR
Division Three. Layer Road. December 1966

FIFA President Stanley Rous was at Loftus Road on the night of 23 August 1966 to switch on the new floodlights, but one man who was there to see him do it had his season plunged into darkness. Bobby Blackwood, Colchester's ex-Hearts winger, had his hopes of winding down to retirement in relatively undemanding fashion in East Anglia cruelly dashed before the first half was over. The details have been sketchily reported, but with nearly 40 minutes gone and Colchester already two goals down, Blackwood "ran into Les Allen's elbow" as one account diplomatically phrased it, and fractured his jaw in two places. That would have been misfortune enough, but the fates – and Allen – weren't finished yet with Blackwood. After 15 games out, the Scot found himself lining up against QPR and Allen again, this time at Layer Road. Twenty minutes in, Blackwood and Allen chased a loose ball into the Colchester penalty area. They went down in a heap, the Colchester player on top. By the time the two were parted, however, Allen was claiming a penalty and Blackwood was once more sporting a broken jaw.

Pain Threshold

5/10

Blackwood gesticulated angrily that the damage had again been done by Allen's elbow, but the Rangers forward, described in one club history as a "neat, ball-playing striker with a quiet temperament", denied there was any intent. If the resulting injury was not as serious as the first – Blackwood had to sit out only nine games this time – the coincidence left him with a sour taste as well as a sore face.

6

Svein Grondalen
Norway v Finland
International friendly. Oslo. August 1980

The Norwegians are a hardy, outdoor people, who like nothing more than skiing vast distances across country, preferably uphill; so strong is their arctic addiction, indeed, that it has been said that they are born with skis on their feet. Of course, Nordic nationals who regularly venture out into the freezing wastelands can prepare themselves for danger, zipping extra rations and a small sleeping bag neatly into their backpacks to avoid the perennial perils of the country's two main natural hazards: landslides and avalanches. Their footballers are unlikely to be buried under a mountain of snow, however, if only because their season runs throughout the northern European summer. Yet there are other threats to a man's safety out there, as Svein Grondalen, a player who made 74 appearances for his country in the 1970s and 1980s, was to discover. Out on a training run with his wife in the Trondheim woods as part of his rehabilitation from injury before a friendly against Finland, the defender was poleaxed by a wandering moose.

Pain Threshold

7/10

High. A Scandinavian centre-back is a fairly fearsome beast, granted, but he is not usually a match *for the average Norwegian elk, which weighs in at about 1500lbs. The myopic mammal is at something of a disadvantage in the survival stakes, however, because it can barely see beyond the points of its own hooves, but Grondalen's knowledge of the fauna of his nation was not sufficient for him to realise he was in no immediate danger and, panicking like a man trying to hack clear a ball from under his own crossbar in the final seconds of extra time, he threw himself down the nearest icy embankment and fractured his hip.*

7

The truth that life can change in a split second became horrifyingly apparent to David Busst a little more than a minute into this game. One moment, the Coventry City defender could see only glory opening before him as the ball broke free in the Manchester United box, the next he was looking at endless months on an operating table as he emerged from a crunching, committed, but perfectly fair challenge with United pair Denis Irwin and Brian McClair, the lower part of his shin hanging by a thread from the rest of his leg. If that was not painful enough, Busst was even to have mementoes of the occasion, the instant of impact being captured by a clump of press photographers and immortalised, if somewhat sickly, in an internet fantasy football league, the Lumpy Sock Conference. Grown men such as Peter Schmeichel and Dion Dublin, who were first on the scene, waved frantically for first aid before turning away, repulsed by the tragedy unfolding before them. It took nine minutes for the paramedics to assess the damage, call in the salvage experts and have Busst hoisted from a pitch by now soaked with blood. Busst never played at professional level again.

Pain Threshold
9/10

Well beyond it, as short-term agony was combined with long-term anguish. Busst, whose name might have given him a clue to his ultimate fate, took to a career in lower-level management and community coaching. But he was not the only one close to the incident to suffer from its after-effects: Schmeichel was so distressed by what he had witnessed, he had to receive counselling from the United club doctor.

8

Steve Morrow
Sheffield Wednesday v Arsenal
League Cup Final, Wembley, April 1993

"It is the bright day that brings forth the adder", is the kind of Shakespearean quotation you are likely to hear Stuart Hall reeling off at the start of one of his sonnets-cum-football reports on Five Live on a Saturday evening, though the Bard probably wasn't thinking of the League Cup Final when he wrote of the potential for pain in the greatest moments. Jumping into the arms of Tony Adams at the final whistle might have seemed a perfectly reasonable way for a match-winning hero to celebrate his finest moment, but Morrow was not to know that his captain's handling was to prove as sure as it had at the wheel of a Ford Sierra XR4 after a boozy barbecue three years earlier. Having hoisted Morrow onto his shoulder, the centre-back seemed to abdicate all responsibility for his team-mate, and allowed the scorer of Arsenal's winning goal to tumble head-first on to the turf, shattering his arm. Stretchered off with an oxygen mask clamped to his face, Morrow missed collecting his winner's medal as well as playing in the following month's FA Cup Final.

Pain Threshold

7/10

Morrow may have been

the one in agony – Ray Parlour revealed afterwards that he had heard the player's arm snap when he hit the ground – but Adams' emotional discomfort was equally severe, and he had to be persuaded to go up and collect the Cup because he felt so bad. Morrow, however, who had a four-inch steel plate containing eight screws inserted into his limb in a three-hour operation, was remarkably reluctant to apportion blame to his skipper. "Tony picked me up and I just lost my balance and came down with a bit of a bump," was his phlegmatic explanation of his predicament.

9

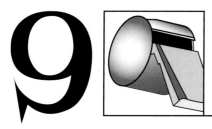

Jimmy Meadows.
Newcastle United v Manchester City.
FA Cup Final. Wembley. May 1955

Things were not looking too promising for Manchester City in the build-up to the showpiece occasion of 1955. Johnny Hart had broken a leg and wouldn't make it, Roy Clarke, scorer of the semi-final winner, was ruled out with a knee problem and Bert Trautmann, the goalkeeper, had developed fibrositis after landing awkwardly in training and was undergoing intensive treatment to ensure he was fit to face the likes of Jackie Milburn. So, when Jimmy Meadows, the talented outside-right, woke up on the morning of the match with a seriously high temperature, it was not entirely for his own reasons that he laughed off suggestions by a nurse that he should think about sitting it out. By the end of the day he was no doubt wishing he had. Turning on the tightly-woven Wembley turf after just 18 minutes, his studs got caught in the grass, and he collapsed with knee ligaments damaged so severely that it was not clear whether the tears that flowed as he was carried to the dressing-room were ones caused by the agony of the injury itself or disappointment at having his big day cut short.

Pain Threshold
8/10

Devastating. It was not just his big day that was curtailed, it was a burgeoning career too. The 24-year-old had recently made his England debut in a 7-2 thrashing of Scotland, but the injury proved so serious that he never played professionally again.

10

Julian Watts and Steve Walsh.
Grimsby Town v Leicester City
League Cup second round.
Blundell Park, October 1997

When Tony Gallimore, the Grimsby full-back, drew back his foot to deliver a long ball into the Leicester area in the 73rd minute of this League Cup tie, he could have had no conception of the havoc that this routine action, carried out hundreds of times throughout the course of a season with varying degrees of success, was to reap. Within an instant, two Leicester players were lying prostrate and in agony, a goalkeeper was sitting on the grass dumbfounded and disconsolate and Steve Livingstone was celebrating a rather fortuitous goal. The trouble started when goalkeeper Kasey Keller and defender Julian Watts each decided to take responsibility for Gallimore's cross. If Keller signalled his intention to come for it, Watts' antennae was not on the right wavelength, and he picked up only a concussed head when the pair collided. From the jumbled mess of limbs in the middle of the penalty area, the ball rebounded onto the unsuspecting shins of Livingstone and dribbled agonisingly towards the empty net. Steve Walsh, facing his own goal, tried to retrieve the situation, but in his efforts to hook his foot round the ball, the Leicester skipper crashed into a post and broke his arm.

Pain Threshold
8 / 10

Grim. Watts and Walsh, on his first game back after four matches on the sidelines, were carted off to hospital, while Livingstone added insult to injuries by bundling home a third four minutes later, giving Second Division Grimsby a surprise win over the holders.

11

Chic Brodie
Colchester United v Brentford
Division Four. Layer Road. November 1970

Even as long ago as 1951 the dangers of being a goalkeeper were well recognised, a survey carried out by the Spanish FA finding that the position produced many more injuries than any other. Chic Brodie bore out the truth of this discovery perhaps better than anybody, the Brentford goalkeeper's luck being so wretched that the only competition he was likely to win was one to be the cover model on a catalogue of disasters. He once survived a hand grenade thrown from the terraces – he scarpered for the touchline and allowed a young police constable to render it harmless – and a collapsing crossbar, but not an excitable small pooch. Finding the turnstiles at Layer Road unguarded, the mongrel slipped into the ground and pushed through the legs of a tightly-packed crowd until he was greeted with a sight that made him think he had died and gone to canine heaven: there, on a wide expanse of muddy earth, were 22 men, all running around and all, seemingly, in pursuit of a ball. Joining in the fun, he eluded all attempts by the groundstaff to catch him, and when Brentford defender Peter Gelson laid a back-pass towards Brodie, the animal showed his pace over ten yards, racing in to upend the goalkeeper as he tried to gather. The mutt yapped, the crowd laughed, but Brodie didn't stir. Carried off on a stretcher, he was found to have serious damage to his knee and played again only in non-league for Margate.

Pain Threshold

9/10

High. Life as a London cabbie seemed to offer an antidote to Brodie's sufferings, but he was right to suspect that the fates were still pursuing him round the backstreets of the capital. So when he crashed into a particularly expensive Jaguar one afternoon he was not surprised to find it jogging his memory of his past life; it was driven by Geoff Hurst.

12

Unused substitute

Wilf Mannion's family on Teesside were devastated when the news came through that the Middlesbrough inside forward had suffered a fatal injury in a collision with Billy Liddell during a home international between England and Scotland at Wembley in April 1951. While they went into grieving mode, it transpired, on closer scrutiny, that someone had misheard the original message and that he had only sustained a facial injury, albeit a mightily unpleasant one – his cheekbone was fractured and there were fears for his eyesight for a while – but at least the mourning dress could be hastily stuffed back in the wardrobe. Mannion may have outwitted the Grim Reaper, but others were not so lucky. Bob Benson,

for example, an Arsenal full-back who was always figuratively willing to burst a blood vessel for any side he represented, did so literally one afternoon in 1916, against Reading, and died shortly after leaving the field. But if Benson, who had been out for ten months, had been brought back too soon, Sam Wynne, a Bury defender whose previous claim to fame had been scoring two goals for each side in a 3-2 victory for former club Oldham over Manchester United in 1923, should have been more circumspect about a touch of the sniffles he experienced before taking the field against Sheffield United four years later. Lining up a free kick, he collapsed suddenly and was carted off to the Bramall Lane dressing-room, where he died of pneumonia.

Chapter Five

The worst refereeing decisions

Worst refereeing decisions

During his tenure as manager of Aston Villa, the otherwise agreeable John Gregory put forward a proposal that has, not altogether surprisingly, yet to be adopted by FIFA. He suggested that referees should have electrodes wired to their genitals and be allowed three poor decisions per match before the plug is attached to the mains. While Gregory was showing plentiful promise for a future career as Home Secretary, Ivano Bonetti, the Italian who took over at Dundee in May 2000, was more personal in his paranoia, the target of his disaffection being Willie Young, an official he was convinced had it in for his team. "As soon as I saw this referee, I knew it would be

2-0 to them," he complained after a match against Motherwell, apparently oblivious to the fact that the game had finished 2-1. "I think he parties every night when Dundee lose". Could Bonetti have had a point: were referees a necessary evil? Or just evil? One scientific survey of the profession provides a chilling answer and gives an insight into how managers, not to mention fans, players and occasionally pundits, can be driven to sanction torture more readily associated with the regime of a banana republic. Its findings imply that, far from coming from a deep-seated desire to see fair play, referees' motivation is more often drawn from a psychological phenomenon the pollsters refer to as "illusory superiority" – in laymen's terms, an "I'm right, you're wrong" syndrome. It is just as well that there is plenty of anecdotal evidence, not to mention that uncovered by the intrusive lens of the television camera, to shatter this illusion. And here are the worst examples of when they have.

1

Urs Meier
Portugal v England
European Championship quarter-finals.
Stadium of Light. June 2004

Graham Poll should have held back on the whistle and waited to see if there was an advantage – but on the morning of this match, he wrote in the *Daily Telegraph* that he was pleased the referees had "barely rated a mention over the past two weeks". For, in the 89th minute of the game, Urs Meier, a veteran of 104 previous internationals, was to nullify much of the good work that had gone before by disallowing Sol Campbell's header, which would almost certainly have won the game for England.

His ruling that John Terry had impeded Portugal goalkeeper Ricardo with the merest brush of an arm was controversial enough for Sven Goran Eriksson, a man not disposed to displays of passion – unless lusty raven-haired secretaries are involved – twice told the Swiss official that it was not a foul.

After England had survived extra time but not the penalty shoot-out that perennially plagues them in serious international competition, Meier took refuge in a telephone call from his girlfriend, also a qualified referee, who assured him of the correctness of his decision. Unfortunately for him, most of England – and especially *Sun* readers – disagreed, and when he accessed his personal website the next morning, he found 16,000 emails drawing his attention to the fact.

Should have gone to Specsavers?

9/10

It wasn't a pair of glasses Meier required but another set of eyes to watch his back. "When I heard English voices, I would look behind me," the terrified official said as The Sun *christened him 'Urs-Hole' and tried to unfurl a giant St George's flag across the front of his house. Being termed an "Emmenthal-eating appeasement monkey" by a* London Evening Standard *columnist was bad enough but when David Mellor, writing in the same paper, was allowed to compare him to a "preening pompadour with the looks of a gay porn star" (how did Mellor know?) he was probably aware it was time to search for another part-time pastime.*

Steven Lodge
Sunderland v Oxford
Division One, Roker Park, February 1993

The earliest referees were equipped not with a whistle but with a white handkerchief, which they would wave to signal a decision; with the unprecedented pressure that comes with the territory these days, they might be better off with a white flag.

Steven Lodge showed an uncommon but frankly laudable tendency to hold up his hands and surrender when his critics pointed out any errors in his ways. Here, he didn't wait for United manager Brian Horton to go wailing to the FA and friendly newspaper reporters, but gave himself up to the authorities without a fight, owning up to his cock-up in his official report to his employers.

But it really was a stinker. Four minutes in and

Terry Butcher's header was saved by Paul Reece, who seemed to be impeded as John Colquhoun's shot from the rebound struck Andy Melville's flailing hand, an action that raised the infamous Roker Roar, not to mention linesman Carl Bassindale's flag. After consulting his assistant, Lodge awarded the penalty, pointed to Mike Ford and, amid furious protests, produced the red card, while Melville kept a low profile. Sunderland had missed two penalties in their previous match, but Don Goodman scored to set them on the way to a 2-0 win.

6/10

Tunnel vision. The result put an end to a tidy little three-match unbeaten run for Oxford, but they were at least able to make the FA see sense once Lodge had reported that on watching the club video afterwards he had realised he had got the wrong man. Although Ford had the blemish wiped off his record, Lodge would later show an ongoing ability to acknowledge his own failings, calling off a match at Gillingham after only six minutes and admitting he should never have started it because the weather was so bad.

3

W R Barnes
Tottenham Hotspur
v Huddersfield Town
Division One, White Hart Lane, April 1952

Tottenham's reputation for playing good football came from the stylish template of Arthur Rowe, the manager who led them to the Second Division championship in 1950 and the title in the top flight a year later. The system, which became known as "push and run", was based on retaining possession, accuracy at a high tempo and the short pass.

It was a break with convention that won many admirers, although it is unlikely that the Huddersfield Town team that struggled throughout the 1951–52 season would have been chief among them – due mainly to a rotten refereeing decision that brought about their defeat at White Hart Lane and contributed to their relegation.

Barnes had just awarded Spurs a corner and had

turned his back on Eddie Baily as the inside-left shaped to take the kick. As Barnes walked along the goalline towards the Huddersfield near post, Baily curled the ball in, only for it to hit the official; it rebounded to Baily, who centred again for Channel Islander Len Duquemin to head home the winner. Huddersfield claimed the goal should not stand because the ball had been played twice by the same player without another touching it, but after consulting with his linesman, Barnes allowed it – then almost immediately blew for full time.

The Yorkshire side demanded a replay, a request turned down by the Football League, and when they took their complaint to a higher authority, they were also disappointed, the FA ruling that although Barnes erroneously thought the ball had been touched by another Tottenham man, his judgement at the time could not be overturned. Charles Buchan, the former England international turned journalist, observing from the stands, called it the "the most amazing decision I have seen in 40 years of football".

4

Laurens van Ravens.
Sporting Lisbon v Rangers
European Cup Winners' Cup. second round second leg. Estadio Jose Alvalade. November 1971

If a referee has notched a World Cup quarter-final on his officiating bedpost, footballers are entitled to think that this is a man whose knowledge of the rule-book can be taken as read. Yet when Laurens van Ravens, who 18 months earlier had taken charge of Uruguay against the Soviet Union in the last eight of Mexico 1970, was chosen to oversee the European Cup Winners' Cup tie between Sporting Lisbon and Rangers, the Scottish side were dumbfounded to discover that he had failed to cast his eye over the small print in the playing conditions.

This crucial oversight came to light only at the end of extra time in the second leg of the tie at the Estadio Jose Alvalade, cost van Ravens his reputation and Rangers, very nearly, a place in the quarter-finals. Rangers had left themselves with much to do after conceding two away goals to the Portuguese side at Ibrox, but had still taken a one-goal advantage to Portugal; twice, on the night, they came from behind but at the end of normal time, as in Glasgow, the score was 3-2 to the home side.

In the ninth minute of extra time, Alfie Conn appeared to have settled things for the Scots; with away goals counting double, his effort left Sporting Lisbon needing two more to triumph, so when the home side grabbed a late penalty, Willie Waddell, the Rangers manager, was not unduly concerned. He should have been. As he prepared to celebrate at the final whistle, van Ravens was preparing for something else altogether: penalties, and when Waddell flourished the contents of Article 3, paragraph 2 of the playing conditions in front of him, he simply waved the Scotsman away. Distracted, the visitors contrived to miss all four of their spot-kicks, while Sporting, who scored two, seemingly advanced.

Should have gone to Specsavers?

5/10

Waddell, Rangers officials and

a UEFA observer went into a locked room to thrash out the situation, while the Scottish Daily Record *put in a call to Hans Bangerter, the UEFA secretary, who explained the confusion – until a recent update, away goals in extra time had not counted double – and assured them that Rangers had triumphed, an outcome trumpeted on the front page of the* Record's *2am edition. Official confirmation was slower to come, by which time one Portuguese newspaper was campaigning for the result to stand on the basis that the referee's decision is final and a delegation from Sporting was chomping at the bit to put their case to UEFA. Bangerter finally provided validation on the Friday and Rangers celebrated by thrashing St Johnstone 4-1 the following day – with three of their goals from penalties.*

5

F Weyland

Ararat Yerevan v West Ham United
European Cup Winners' Cup, Second round, first leg, Kotayk Stadium, October 1976

They didn't quite go in two by two, but the West Ham supporters who travelled to the Armenian town that sits at the foot of Mount Ararat, on which Noah's Ark is fabled to have come to rest, were a rare enough species to have attracted the attention of a man charged by his creator with rejuvenating civilisation – there were only 45 of them to admire a stadium that resembled a Roman amphitheatre. And to add insult to injury, the Hammers brought with them a team of caterers and a plentiful supply of non-Soviet food, no doubt including a bumper package of jellied eels.

The stunt backfired, however, when Trevor Brooking

swallowed something slippery and was ruled out with a stomach complaint. West Ham's troubles didn't end there, either, thanks to a West German referee with a tenuous grasp of the rules. First, the official saw no reason to blow for a foul when Mervyn Day was barged in mid-air as he tried to gather a high centre from the right wing. Nor, when Ararat forward Samuel Petrosian headed the ball from Day's hands and slotted it into the net for the equaliser, did he activate his whistle, later claiming it was a perfectly good goal because the goalkeeper had dropped the ball.

Should have gone to Specsavers?

 6/10

When West Ham manager Ron Greenwood questioned this version of events, Weyland changed his story, saying that Day had been tossing the ball from hand to hand when Petrosian made his move.

6

Roy Capey
Chelsea v Ipswich
Division One. Stamford Bridge. September 1970

Roy Capey was a fully-paid-up member of the Referee is Always Right Club. When, in the 63rd minute, Alan Hudson picked up a pass from Peter Houseman, and hammered in a shot from 25 yards that appeared to slide along the side netting, hit the stanchion and creep into the back corner of the goal, Capey chose to ignore the testimony of 38,000 pairs of eyes – the Chelsea fans clapped Hudson's effort but did not cheer a goal – and several more besides, among them a BBC cameraman right behind the goal, a police inspector stationed nearby, and Ipswich goalkeeper David Best, who innocently retrieved the ball and placed it in readiness for a goal kick.

Instead, and to everyone's astonishment, the referee pointed to the centre spot to signal that Chelsea had taken a 2-0 lead. Even when persuaded by the apoplectic Ipswich players to consult his linesman, Capey could not be convinced to see sense, and although Bobby Robson's side sneaked a consolation, they were left to contact the PFA to lobby on their behalf for their draw bonus. The disconsolate Ipswich players were left to troop off to the caustic comments of the home club's PA announcer: "As far as we know, Chelsea won 2–1."

Should have gone to Specsavers?

8/10

Fired by righteous

indignation, a mostly sympathetic Chelsea dressing-room – Hudson was a lone dissenter, suggesting: "If the ref said it went in that's what counts" – and a shoal of supportive letters from Chelsea fans, Robson pressed his claims with the Football League for a replay. But Alan Hardaker, the league's secretary, was to prove as immovable as his predecessors and, working on the premise that two wrongs make a right, noted: "There was not half the fuss when Newcastle beat Arsenal in the 1932 FA Cup final with a goal that later proved not to be one."

7

Actually, Hardaker's contention that there was "not much fuss" when Newcastle beat Arsenal with the help of a controversial goal 38 years previously is not completely true and, hard though it may be to believe about an era in which television was barely in its infancy, technology was to be called upon to refute claims of refereeing infallibility.

Thus, when Bill Harper said after the match, which the Magpies won 2-1, that the first of their goals, which levelled the scores in the 38th minute, was perfectly fair "as God is my judge", he found himself subject to the appraisal of something that, if not quite as omniscient as the Almighty, was in the right place at the right time: the British Movietone News.

It revealed in glorious black and white that the ball was clearly over the dead-ball line when Jimmy Nicholson whipped it across for Jack Allen, surprised to find himself free from a challenge from an Arsenal defence already preparing for a goal kick, to nod home. It also helped to dispel Harper's notion that he had been close enough to the incident to judge. "I was eight yards away and I know what I saw," he said, despite the evidence of the film showing him a good 25 yards distant.

Should have gone to Specsavers?

8/10

Would have helped if another form of technology – laser treatment – had been available to Mr Harper. Allen added the winner 18 minutes from time and when a Dixie Dean-inspired Everton grabbed the league title, Arsenal had seen a possible double snatched from under their noses. Don't laugh.

In October 1919, Freddie Groves, the Arsenal inside-right, hit a long shot that cannoned against the Everton crossbar, bounced down in front of the goal-line and was cleared to safety. When the referee surprised everyone at Highbury by awarding a goal, it no doubt pleased Groves – he scored only five others in a 50-game career for the Gunners – as much as it galled the Mersysiders, who spent the next few minutes pumping the ball repeatedly into touch in a collective fit of pique.

The example is presented to show that controversies over whether the ball has crossed the line are by no means a modern phenomenon and that Mark Clattenburg is by no stretch of the imagination the first referee to find himself at the centre of such controversies. But when he failed to give a goal after Manchester United keeper Roy Carroll fumbled Pedro Mendes' speculative lob-shot from close to the centre circle over the line before clawing it back and acting as if nothing untoward had happened, he was the first to be quite so swiftly and comprehensively condemned by technology – even the Azerbaijani linesman in the 1966 World Cup final was given several decades' grace before scientists had in their hands the requisite instrumentation to suggest Geoff Hurst's second goal should not have been given.

Should have gone to Specsavers?

9/10

Before Clattenburg and his assistant Rob Lewis had left the field following the 90th-minute incident, television viewers, not to mention many behind Carroll's goal, knew that Tottenham had been robbed. But Martin Jol, the Spurs manager, was surprisingly phlegmatic about the decision afterwards – perhaps a point from a goalless draw at a ground where they had not won since 1989 was in itself cause for celebration – while Sir Alex Ferguson sought to deflect criticism of his goalkeeper by pointing to a penalty appeal that United had had turned down. Lewis, who had been level with the last defender, suggested he would have had to have had the legs of Linford Christie to have been in a position to see the goal clearly, while journalists and pundits called for a weird variety of objects – from a computerised chip to a klaxon or bell – to be placed in the ball to indicate when it had crossed the line.

9

David Elleray
Chesterfield v Middlesbrough
FA Cup semi-final. Old Trafford. April 1997

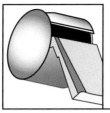

Cup fever can do curious things to a club, especially if it comes from the lower divisions. When Chesterfield, a club whose town was famous for its crooked church spire, came within 90 minutes of another architectural oddity – Wembley's twin towers – the people could not be contained, happily accommodating the national press when they descended in numbers to write patronising articles about them, gleefully purchasing the team's Cup-run song in preference to a chart-topping Spice Girls effort and coughing up the regulation fiver to have

their photo taken with the Cup when it was motored up the M1 for the day.

But some more sober individuals were more restrained in their revelry, seeing the latter event as tempting fate. And their concerns were realised midway through the second half when David Elleray made two decisions that bewildered the 22,500 Chesterfield fans who had travelled to Manchester for the occasion, as well as millions more willing on the underdogs from in front of their TV sets.

First, in the 70th minute, when Jon Howard's shot from six yards cannoned down from the bar, bounced over the line and came out again, instead of awarding a goal he blew for a free kick against Andy Morris, who was trying to force the ball back in again – Elleray was perfectly positioned for the foul, it seemed, but not the goal that preceded it by a fraction of a second – and then, moments later, when Sean Dyche obstructed Juninho seemingly outside the box at the other end, he pointed to the penalty spot.

As Craig Hignett joyously despatched the kick, Chesterfield had seen a prospective 3–1 scoreline in their favour become a 2–2, and although they were to secure a 3–3 draw after extra-time, their best chance had gone and they slipped to a single-goal defeat in the replay.

Should have gone to Specsavers?

8/10

Elleray later claimed he had awarded the free-kick before Howard's shot, but Chesterfield were unhappy that he didn't say who committed the foul or why he had taken so long to signal it.

10

Byron Moreno
Barcelona de Guayaquil v Deportiva Universitaria Quito
Ecuadorian League, Estadio Monumental
Isidro Romero Carbo, September 2002

Controversy attaches itself to some referees like a competent man-to-man marker keeping tabs on his most dangerous opponent. Byron Moreno first came to attention for his officiating at the 2002 World Cup, where he upset the Italians so much during their defeat by South Korea – he awarded the co-hosts a penalty, sent off Francesco Totti and disallowed a 'golden goal' by Damiano Tomassi – that they were moved to name a public toilet after him.

But he found himself even deeper in the mire

after a league game in his native Ecuador, where Deportiva Universitaria Quito were trailing 3–2 until Moreno took 'Fergie time' into a new realm of physics by signalling an additional six minutes, then adding on 13, in the last three of which Deportiva conveniently scored twice. The extension only aroused serious suspicions when it was pointed out that Moreno was running for mayor in Quito.

Should have gone to Specsavers?

10/10

No, but perhaps he should have made a beeline for the nearest jewellers to have his watch repaired. Moreno, who had been given a standing ovation at his first domestic match on his return from the Far East, remained defiant despite being banned for 20 matches by the Ecuadorean football federation, who found him guilty of including "false facts" in his match report.

11

Albert Tejada
Argentina v Brazil
Copa America quarter-finals.
Atilio Paiva Olivera, Uruguay, July 1995

The Hand of God works in mysterious ways and, if English folk are inclined to believe that the Almighty is an Argentinian after Diego Maradona palmed in the opening goal in the 1986 World Cup quarter-final between the teams, they will at least be gratified to know that He made good on his promise that you reap what you sow, even though it took a whole nine years. Argentina, 2-1 in the lead, were only eight minutes away from the semi-finals of the Copa America when Tulio, the Brazil forward, almost literally snatched the place from them. Unlike

Maradona, his attempt on goal was perfectly legal but his control – he brought the ball down with his hand – was not, a fact obvious to all in the ground, apart from Albert Tejada, the Peruvian referee, and his linesman, the suspiciously English-sounding Colombian Daniel Wilson. The game went to extra time and then penalties, the villain of the piece Tulio notching one of the spot kicks as Brazil ran out 4-2 winners.

Should have gone to Specsavers?

7/10

The matter rose to presidential level back in Buenos Aires, where Carlos Menem branded the victory a "monumental robbery", casting further aspersions on Tejada's abilities by claiming that the goal was not just handball but offside as well. While Brazil celebrated the 'Hand of Tulio', Argentinean newspapers hissed supernaturally about the 'Hand of the Devil'.

12 Unused substitute

The royal patronage afforded to Real Madrid and, later, the support of Franco, have given the club a firm sense of superiority – one perhaps most regularly questioned by Barcelona, whose main response to the capital's snootiness has been to express their sense of regional identity in their trendiness. But if the pair had a history of fierce rivalry, it was made all the more fierce by a history of dubious refereeing decisions, most of which, the Catalan side felt, had gone the way of their great adversary. Most recently that misfortune manifested itself in a decision by Jose Losantos Omar that Joan Gaspart, the Barcelona president, likened to being "mugged of his wallet". Losantos Omar ruled out what would have been an injury-time winner for offside, despite the ball having clipped the ankles of Real's Ivan Helguera last, thus playing two Barcelona players onside. But if Barcelona think that they have received the thin end of the wedge from Spanish officials, when things have turned in their favour, they have done so with a vengeance. In 1960, they were drawn to face their old enemy, champions of the Continent for the previous five seasons, in the second round of the European Cup. When, trailing 2-1 in the first leg at the Bernabeu, Evaristo, Barcelona's Brazilian forward, received the ball in a clear offside position, English referee Arthur Ellis inexplicably waved play on. Evaristo advanced, was felled, or dived, depending on your allegiance, and Barcelona took a second away goal with them back to the Nou Camp. Yet if Madrid felt hard done by at home, they were to feel as if there was an English conspiracy against them in the return match. The bare statistics record a 2-1 victory to Barcelona, but tell nothing of the controversy behind it: Reg Leafe no doubt had his reasons for disallowing four Madrid goals, but years later, when the television pictures were subject to critical analysis, experts could not confirm them.

Chapter Six

The worst chairmen and club owners

The worst chairmen

Football hooligans? "There are the 92 club chairmen for a start," said Brian Clough, articulating in one succinct phrase what many fans feel about the men who run their clubs. From the cigar-chomping local dignitary with an ego two sizes too big to fit inside his sheepskin coat, to the breed of younger, sharp-suited multinational businessmen with a couple of holiday homes in the Bahamas and a set of accounts offshore, they are, in the main, people

and club owners

you wouldn't want to be forced to share a lift with in a two-storey building, let alone have as company for most of your Saturday afternoons. One (honest) chairman once commented that football is a charity, not a business, but few have seen it that way and, far from using their position to lead their fans into the promised land, have used it to beef up their bank balances or restore them when their investments have taken a turn for the worse. Trailing in the wake of these individuals, some misguided, some megalomaniac and others, frankly, villainous, have been clubs stripped of their assets, with no proper home to call their own or saddled with debt.

1  Charles Koppel, Bjorn Gjelsten and Kjell Inge Rokke

A couple of years after acquiring the club with Kjell Inge Rokke, a fellow Norwegian and billionaire fishing magnate, with a promise from outgoing Wimbledon owner Sam Hammam that he could make them the Dublin Dons, Bjorn Gjelsten, finding that the Irish FA were unwilling to rubber-stamp the move, seemed resigned to having to return the 1988 FA Cup winners to their old stamping ground in the London Borough of Merton.

"If we end up in Milton Keynes or Oslo, something will have gone dramatically wrong," he told *Four Four Two* magazine with a straight face, before planting South African solicitor Charles Koppel in the chairman's seat and instructing him to deliver a way out through Buckinghamshire. When Koppel caught wind of the fact that Wimbledon fans had drawn up a report showing that a return from Selhurst Park to Plough Lane was not just feasible but favoured by a large majority in SW19 – not to mention not particularly pricey for two of the richest men in Scandinavia – he sprang into damage limitation mode.

Persuading a hitherto unknown residents' association to meet him in secret, he attempted to rally them into a fighting force capable of obstructing efforts to return the club to their doorstep. Unfortunately for a man so steeped in football lore that he was unaware that Sheffields Wednesday and United were separate clubs, Koppel underestimated the supporters' intelligence – in both senses of the word – unwittingly allowing a Womble agent to infiltrate the covert gathering and record what should have ranked as one of the biggest football public relations faux-pas of recent times. Or would have done if anyone in the newspaper world had chosen to report it.

Cigar of Choice

9/10

Slim Panatellas all round.

None of the trio seemed comfortable in the public eye, preferring to follow their hobby of powerboat racing than attend meetings they had arranged with fans' representatives. But Koppel was there when it really mattered, using the smooth-talk he had learned in the legal trade to convince the fellow lawyer who chaired an FA Commission set up to rule on the move that Wimbledon would have to go into administration if they didn't. Fans pointed to the club's reputation as a selling entity, surviving on transfer fees for years, but it cut little tobacco with the panel and the peculiar entity that is the Milton Keynes Dons was born.

Terry Smith
Chester City

When Terry Smith breezed into the Deva Stadium in the middle of the 1999 close season, Chester City fans, their club deep in administration and on the brink of going out of business, could have been forgiven for thinking that they had found a saviour – though in truth it was Smith's father's money that had bought him a football club of his own to play with.

Smith arrived trailing a resumé decorated with championships, trophies and medals from his career in football. Unfortunately, it was American football. Before long, Kevin Ratcliffe, the manager, had left the club and Smith had sacked the chief executive and academy director – both would later take him to employment tribunals – and installed himself in the dugout.

Reneging on an agreement to run the club in partnership with the fans, he refused to acknowledge the differences between association football and the gridiron game, selecting three captains – dee-fence, midfield, and offence – and practising scrimmages in training. It had to end in tears, and it did as Smith was as good as his promise to take Chester where they'd never been before: sadly,

it was the Conference, after a stay in league football of 69 years.

Cigar of Choice

8/10

A Corona, with a rounded but closed head, somewhat like the balding Smith's. A clue that his American dream would soon turn into a nightmare might have been found in his admission that he had originally bought the club because he was taken with Chester Zoo.

3

Ken Richardson
Doncaster Rovers

SAS soldiers are trained to cover their tracks, even going so far as to poop scoop their own faeces off the desert floor and pop it into a small compartment in their backpacks to keep the Republican Guard off their trail. So when Ken Richardson, the Doncaster Rovers owner, enlisted the help of Alan Kristiansen, supposedly a former member of the secretive Hereford-based regiment, to burn down the Belle Vue main stand in an attempt to realise the value of the ground for development, the last thing he would have expected him to do was leave behind any incriminating evidence. Especially not in the form of a mobile phone, abandoned among the charred remains of the building, which revealed that the last call the stupid ex-squaddie had made had been to his employer's answerphone, on which he had left the unmistakeable message: "It's done boss." On the contrary, the only thing that was done was the dim-witted Kristiansen – and his flabbergasted gaffer once the police persuaded the former soldier to turn chief witness for the prosecution in Richardson's trial for conspiracy to commit arson.

Cigar of Choice

9/10

Diadema, an eight-inch whopper almost as big as the porkies Richardson was prepared to tell. It was nearly four years before the case came to trial, during which time Richardson presided over rapidly plummeting fortunes that saw the club's debts increase ten-fold and managers come and go with startling regularity. By the time Doncaster dropped into the Conference at the end of the 1997-8 season, Richardson, who a decade earlier had been warned off racecourses by the Jockey Club for his involvement in the Flockton Grey horse-racing scandal, defied his status as a waste-paper magnate by refusing to attend matches on the basis that he "didn't want to be associated with rubbish".

4

Lt Col Thomas Gibson-Poole
Middlesbrough

ony Blair may have claimed to have sat in the Gallowgate End at Newcastle cheering on 'Wor Jackie' Milburn – unlikely, as the Gallowgate was a terrace at the time and Blair was still in nappies when Milburn left – but he is not the first politician in the North East to have used football to try to improve his election prospects.

Most notable among these was Lt Col Thomas Gibson-Poole, the Middlesbrough chairman, who thought that his chances of securing the constituency for the Conservatives in the 1911 general election could be bolstered by the feel-good factor a victory for his team over Sunderland, at that time the only unbeaten club in the league, would create.

Yet Gibson-Poole, like so many of those who lust

after power, did not want to get his own hands dirty, and persuaded Andy Walker, a manager already under investigation for alleged illegal approaches to players at his former club Airdrie, to carry out the deed. The Scotsman buttonholed Sunderland's captain before the match and offered £30 – a tenner for the skipper and £2 for each of the rest of the team – for the Wearsiders to lose the encounter. Stunned, Charlie Thomson went straight to his chairman, and a complaint was lodged with the FA.

Cigar of Choice

8/10

An unravelled Culebras.

Boro, the bad apples of English football, were proving rotten to the core: Gibson-Poole, the town's mayor, had only just taken over when 11 board members had been suspended over financial irregularities. He protested his innocence, threatening legal action against his accusers, but along with Walker was found guilty and banned from the game for life.

5

Eurico Miranda
Vasco de Gama

Eurico Miranda is big, fat, and very bad news for journalists. While most club chairmen have had their run-ins with reporters – a harsh word here, an indeterminate ban from the press box there for the offending hack – Miranda once took it a step further, warning newshounds that the club would not be responsible for the security of any of their ilk caught penning critical comments. Some defied the Vasco president, attending the club's Sao Januario stadium with personal policemen in tow, but it didn't prevent Jose Carlos Araujo, one of the country's most respected radio commentators, getting a cup of urine thrown over him.

If that was taking the piss, Miranda was blatant in his admission of doing so further by rigging the poll to get his yes-men alongside him on the ruling council in the club's 2000 elections. And when Pele, as Minister of Sport, tried to pass a bill that would bring about greater transparency in the game, Miranda, also a member of Congress, lobbied so successfully against it that by the time it reached the statute book it was reduced to 11 per cent of its original wording.

Cigar of Choice

7/10

Usually to be seen with a revolting fat Robusto stubbed between his smug lips, he generally removes it only to shout obscenities at the referee. Loved by Vasco fans in direct proportion to the amount he is loathed by everyone else, he once sacked a manager for embracing an opposition coach in a spirit of fair play.

6

Stan Flashman
Barnet

Flash, and supremely well-fed to go with it, the original Loadsamoney was never comfortable unless he had several seats to himself and an enormous wad of cash protruding from his back pocket. The self-styled ticket broker – tout or spiv to his enemies, and there were enough of those that he was once handcuffed and gagged by rivals and relieved of his plentiful supply of FA Cup final tickets – was at first welcomed by Barnet supporters when his financial input of £50,000 saved the club from receivership in 1985.

But even as the club rose to the Football League under Barry Fry's management, Flashman was accountable to no-one, throwing opposition directors out of the boardroom if he thought their team had been too dirty, threatening to break the legs of Barnet players he didn't rate, or sacking Fry in a rage before reappointing him when he'd cooled down.

And when things started to go wrong, he didn't spare those who had initially fêted him, saying "the fans don't matter to me" and warning one female follower that he would "permanently mark her face" if she kept criticising him. This law unto himself finally found the authorities closing in on him after players went unpaid and testimonial monies vanished without trace in 1992.

Cigar of Choice

6/1o

Several boxes of Cubans, smuggled through the red channel to avoid paying duty. By the end, practically everyone – the Inland Revenue, VAT officials and the fraud squad – was on

Flashman's trail, and Barnet, their future again in doubt, were beginning the downward spiral back to the Conference. Flashman was declared bankrupt, avoided a court appearance only on health grounds, and swapped his palatial home in Totteridge for a terrace in Ilford. But Fry, who was left short by £162,000, was surprisingly generous in his appraisal of the big man. "Anyone who didn't know Stanley would have thought he was an ignorant pig," he said. "But if he hadn't come into the club it would not have known the success it did."

7

Keith Cheeseman
Dunstable Town

Barry Fry suffered two heart attacks while dealing with the stressful Flashman at Barnet, but chairmen who aroused unnaturally intense interest among the country's constabularies were a recurring theme in the early part of his managerial career. Offered his first job at a desperately underachieving Dunstable Town, eight successive years bottom of the Southern League, his ticker missed a beat or two when Keith Cheeseman parked his red sports car outside the dilapidated building that passed for Fry's office and blew through the door, looking every inch the successful businessman in pin-striped suit and inordinately wide 1970s collars, and brandishing blank cheques that Fry was encouraged to fill in when he'd identified his transfer targets.

Fry's suspicions were first kindled when his chairman frisked a subsequent arrival for firearms. Three days later, when Cheeseman ordered Fry to deliver to him, by a circuitous route, a case stuffed full of foreign currency, the 28-year-old player-manager sensed he was up to his knees in something messy, a feeling confirmed when his wife phoned to inform him that there were armed men in the bushes of a neighbour's garden.

Cigar of Choice

6/10

A Pyramid, probably half-inched. The readies that Cheeseman always had poking from every orifice were found to have a source closer to home than international business deals: the Dunstable players and their families. The chairman had obtained personal details from them all by inviting them to the Christmas party and then applying for loans in their names. Jailed for six years, he was later tailed by the FBI in an investigation into money laundering. Jumping bail, he was thought to have suffered a grisly fate when a headless body was found in a lay-by. However, he showed his face again after Fry took over at Peterborough, but the board were not interested in his financial input.

8

Jesus Gil
Atletico Madrid

"**S**on of a whore!" "No, you're the son of a whore!" "The only son of a whore is you, you clown!" Traditional greetings can come in many forms and, although it obviously loses something in translation from its original tongue, this was the essence of the pleasantries exchanged when Jesus Gil y Gil, the owner of Atletico Madrid, came face-to-face with his counterpart from Compostela, Jose Maria Caneda, outside the Spanish FA one day in April 1996.

Gil had been enraged some days earlier when Caneda had gone on record as criticising the residents of Marbella for electing Gil as mayor – and to be honest, anyone who votes for a man campaigning on a promise of constructing more cheap housing despite once being imprisoned over the collapse of a restaurant roof his company had built (58 people died, but General Franco later pardoned him) probably needs to have their wisdom questioned.

The king of the Costa del Crime rode a coach and horses through legislation, and an elephant on the pitch to celebrate Atletico's league and cup double success. Big-name managers came and went – a dozen of them between 1987 and 1994 – while Gil retained rights of veto on team, tactics and transfers… and then boasted that sacking a coach was as simple as sipping a sweet sherry.

Cigar of Choice

8/10

More a beer and wine man – and a wildly creative accountant to boot: an investigation showed that he had diverted public funds in Marbella into the club, from which he was later found to have defrauded many millions.

9

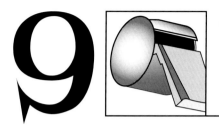

Bill Archer, Greg Stanley and David Bellotti
Brighton and Hove Albion

Take one businessman with no known interest in football. Add his business partner, a Chelsea fan best known for kicking in a shop window in Doncaster and getting fined. Mix in a former MP with no previous experience of the game. Oh, and one of those prime pieces of real estate known to the naïve fans as a football ground. The failed politician, David Bellotti, becomes chief executive with a remit that consists of looking after the interests of the share-holders – the aforementioned businessmen, Lancastrian Bill Archer, who has bought control of the club in question, Brighton & Hove Albion, for a princely £56.25, and Greg Stanley. Those interests are best served, they believe, by selling the piece of real estate, the Goldstone Ground, home of the Seagulls for nearly 100 years. The deal is conducted in secret. There are no realistic plans for a new stadium, and the scheme involves ground-sharing, many miles away in a different county. Two years of civil war follow. The trio become the most hated men in Sussex, and are burned in effigy by the local bonfire society. The team drops rapidly towards the Conference. The terraces are in constant uproar.

Cigar of Choice

9/10

The full Fidel, lovingly rolled on the perfectly-formed thigh of a dusky Havana maiden while the guilty men sip Daiquiris (or, in Stanley's case, gulp down pints of the sticky liquid) and discuss their latest property deals. The club is taken over, and it survives relegation on the final day of the season. But the ground has gone. It fetches £7.4million; it's later sold on. For £24million.

10

Bernard Tapie
Marseilles

Gallic panache, as shown by the likes of Thierry Henry, Michel Platini, David Ginola, and Zinedine Zidane in recent decades, may be crucial in prising open the most stubborn of rearguards, but it can be less helpful when it is the defences of such players under the cosh.

Thus, when authorities began their investigation into the Marseilles match-fixing scandal of 1993 – president Bernard Tapie and his managing director Jean-Pierre Bernes were accused of offering bribes to Valenciennes players to lose a league game days before leaders Marseilles became the first French team to win the European Cup – it was the skilful ones, considered most mentally vulnerable to a couple of hours of hard interrogation, on whom they focused first.

After they cracked, one by one signing confessions to their roles in the saga, it was downhill all the way, Tapie finding his cast-iron alibis collapsing. First, Valenciennes coach Boro Primorac, later to become Arséne Wenger's assistant at Arsenal, admitted that Tapie had offered him a pay-off and a coaching post at Second Division

Martigues if he was willing to take the blame; then Jean-Jacques Eydelie, the Marseilles player who offered the opposition bribes on behalf of his bosses, revealed all from his remand cell, and Bernes himself finally owned up but fingered Tapie as the mastermind.

Cigar of Choice

9/10

The Marseilles public choked on their Gitanes, although observers among them were quick to point to a more sinister element to Tapie's prosecution: his success in business – he'd grown rich by taking over ailing companies; in politics – he was a socialist and member of the European Parliament; and in sport – where Marseilles had won five consecutive championships. He was imprisoned, others received suspended sentences, and Marseilles, the biggest club in the country, were thrown out of the European Cup – costing them 450 million francs – and demoted to the Second Division. But Tapie couldn't be kept off the big stage for long: on release he became an actor, starring in a French translation of One Flew Over The Cuckoo's Nest.

11

Robert Maxwell
Oxford United

For a man whose birthplace was known variously as Slatinske Doly, Szlastina, Aknazlatina and Solotvino, and at different times belonged to the Hungarians, Czechs and Polish before being absorbed into the former Soviet Union at the end of the Second World War, it is hardly surprising that Robert Maxwell (the British name he settled on after forging earlier identities as Jan Hoch and Abraham Lieb) found it difficult to appreciate the differences between Oxford and Reading, even the obvious one that the cities were 25 miles apart.

Thus, not so long after acting as local hero, investing £125,000 from his base in nearby Headington Hall to save the Manor Ground outfit, he was moving from acquisition to merger mode, announcing that the clubs – he also had a shareholding in Reading – would combine in a regional perversion to be known as the Thames Valley Royals.

The Bouncing Czech, once considered by the DTI to be "unfit" to be a company director, did manage to unite the two sets of supporters – against him. By a neat coincidence, the second game after the announcement brought the sides together on the pitch, and along with the widespread anti-merger banners on display, the fans joined forces with a chanted message that left Maxwell in no doubt that he was no longer welcome around those parts.

But it was the intervention of Roger Smee that proved critical. The business-man linked up with three dissenting Reading directors to block Royals' chair-man Frank Waller from transferring his shareholding to Maxwell, forcing him to abandon the deal. He returned to his usual games of raiding pension funds and floating companies, but discovered that he himself wasn't quite as good at floating, fatally falling off his boat as the net closed around him in 1991.

Cigar of Choice

8/10

For a man awarded the military cross by General Montgomery, as he often liked to remind people, nothing would suffice but a Churchill, whose trademark puffing gave the name to the 7-incher. Thwarted in the Thames Valley, Maxwell turned his attentions to Manchester United but found the £15 million asking price too steep, instead paying £300,000 for a debt-ridden Derby County, asset-stripping Dean Saunders from Oxford to lead the Rams' attack, and installing son Ian as chairman. Attempts to purchase Watford and buy influence at Tottenham were opposed by the Football League and frustrated his interest in the game.

12 Unused substitute

The old phrase goes that those who can't do, teach. When Michael Knighton found he was not good enough to be a footballer, he not surprisingly turned to education, passing on his expertise in geography and PE to the children at a private school in Huddersfield. But he didn't lose his dream, and in 1989, supported by a lucrative sideline in property development and a couple of wealthy businessmen, he put in operation a plan to buy Manchester United, at the time a slumbering giant, from Martin Edwards for a measly fee, in hindsight, of just over £10million. Knighton had his moment in the sun, introducing himself to the Stretford End with a few keepie-uppies on the Old Trafford pitch before slamming the ball into the net in front of them, but the deal fell through, although he sat on the board for a couple of years. Tiring of that, Knighton went from the sublime to the ridiculous, setting his sights on Carlisle United, who had just finished 92nd out of 92 Football League teams. But the moustachioed mystic had a vision – and not the one of little green men hovering over the M62 in their magnificent unidentified flying machine that was to earn him widespread media ridicule when it was revealed in the *Carlisle News and Star* some years later (he claimed the comments had been off the record). He predicted a Premier League presence in Cumbria within a decade, but as the club yo-yoed between the bottom two divisions and the proposed redevelopment of Brunton Park went uncompleted, the Carlisle faithful lost, well, faith, especially when they found that his main forecast, that one day the club would be able to pay him a "gargantuan" salary, had already come true. He tried to sell off his shares in the club, but found no takers – and after he was forced out when the club went into administration, 10,000 fans turned up for the first game of the next season to celebrate his going.

Chapter Seven

The worst fans

The worst fans

It is not an uncommon occurrence to witness a professional footballer singing the praises of his team's fans – usually, two days before he signs a four-year contract with their biggest rivals up the road. In the game's equivalent of the telephone voice, he will earnestly intone about how "they're a great set of fans here, they deserve the best", before slipping out of the players' entrance, ignoring small boys' requests for autographs and screeching away in his £90,000 Lamborghini Convertible (special edition), leaving those who only hours earlier were chanting his name in unison to stare at his personalised number-plate as it disappears into the distance. But for all those who don't deserve this sort of treatment for their loyal contributions to his pay packet, there are others who even the most amenable manager wouldn't want round for dinner – and we are not just talking here about the hooligans, the homophobes, the xeno-phobes and the bloke whose backside is so colossal he starts to take up residence in your seat as well as his own. Just as there are defenders who would hack down their own grandmothers if her advance on the penalty area was threatening their win bonus, agents who would demand commission for collecting her pension from the post office and managers who would want her back on the field within hours of her hip replacement operation, so there are the supporting equivalents; you probably know your team's, you have almost certainly heard them or, most scarily of all, you may even be one...

Mark Glanville
Manchester United

The football world has generally given hooligans a bad press – but there has been one sector of society that refuses to condemn men who wouldn't think twice before shoving a broken bottle into your laughing gear as you sup your pre-match pint: the book industry. In fact, in an act for which society can perhaps be grateful, the leading publishing houses, and some more dubious ones, have helped these wayward individuals find a new outlet for their aggression: the printed word.

The shelves of Waterstones and WH Smith's are brimful of the brothers Brimson and heaving under a hundredweight of Headhunters. Of the many, but not very varied, accounts of this bovversome bunch, there is one that stands out, and that is the tale of Mark Glanville, a Cockney Red who added to his not inconsiderable crimes by becoming a singer with the Lisbon Opera.

The clash of cultures suggested by the two activities is not quite as resounding as it might be: Glanville was no product of a deprived inner city estate, but as middle-class as they come, only being taken to his first Manchester United game as a treat for passing his clarinet grade 5 exam, and he had to work hard over a number of years to win true acceptance from his new mates.

Terrace Terror

5/10

More like terrace tenor.

2

Unknown Manchester City fans
Manchester United v Manchester City
FA Cup fifth round. Old Trafford. March 1996

While personal emails given out by national newspapers can prove a helpful shortcut these days, in the past the Royal Mail would usually provide a speedy service should you wish to put on record your grievance with a particular refereeing decision. A letter addressed with the official's name and home town would, like those sent simply to Santa, Lapland, find its intended target. Sometimes, as Alan Wilkie, the referee in this match was to find out, the FA would oblige by forwarding it themselves.

Thus, having awarded a controversial penalty that ensured a 2-1 victory for the home side, Wilkie was not particularly surprised to be bombarded by correspondence from a number of disaffected City supporters, some drawing on their favourite one-liners to inform him that "a bullet is waiting for you at Maine Road", where he could expect a deatn slow and, like an Alan Parry commentary, immensely painful. All the wordsmiths were, of course, anonymous. Except for one. Having launched into a scribbled diatribe on how Wilkie had spoiled his little boy's birthday treat as he had intended to take him to Wembley for the final – if nothing else, demonstrating the eternal optimism that lies within City fans' hearts – the writer obligingly concluded by signing and addressing it.

Terrace Terror

3/10

Nasty, but ultimately stupid. Wilkie simply dispatched the letter to Manchester CID, who were not unduly tested in tracing the man, and the ringleaders of the hate campaign were rounded up.

175

3

Backing your club through the very hardest of times is no mean task, attendances plummeting at the very whisper of the 'r' word, but those who stick with it must be prepared for masochism of the highest order. Sometimes though, the very act of fandom can be detrimental to the constitution.

At around the time physicians in Italy were claiming to have found scientific proof of the malignant effects on mental health of the supporting life – 'mal de Fiorentina' they called an illness they had identified in the fans of Florence's Serie A side – Leicester City follower Tommy Tyrrell was claiming to be suffering from a similar malady.

After taking two days off work to recover from Mike Reed's controversial award of an extra-time penalty that handed Chelsea this hard-fought tie on a plate – the first official case of post-traumatic ref disorder – the Foxes' follower decided some recompense was required. Encouraged by some ambulance-chasing lawyers, and backed by the fanzine *Where's The Money Gone?* (probably on legal costs) he revealed his plan to sue the FA for loss of earnings.

Terrace Terror

4/10

Legally flawed. The absence of subsequent newspaper reports on the progress of the action suggests that Tyrrell, a man for whom this defeat was "like losing a close friend", thought better of it after studying the small type. He might have been influenced by the letter writer to The Times who cited a similar case in rugby (Spolding versus Whitworth if you can be bothered) in which the Court of Appeal ruled that officials could be held liable only for a player's safety, not for errors of judgment made in a split second. In separate but amusing postscripts, Danny Baker was sacked from Radio Five Live's 6-0-6 programme for suggesting grieving supporters should make unsolicited visits to Mr Reed's abode, while Reed got in on the litigious action himself some months later, threatening to sue John Hartson after the West Ham striker had made reference to his "s***house decision making" – during a controversial defeat. Against Leicester.

4

Derrick Arnott
Middlesbrough
December 1997

As a retired insurance executive, Derrick Arnott would have been well aware that you can cover for pretty much every eventuality, Acts of God excepted. And when the roof fell in on his world – that is, Middlesbrough were relegated from the Premiership at the end of the 1996-97 season – he was sure that no supernatural hands were at work.

In fact, he laid the blame squarely at the door of far more fallible hands – mainly those belonging to the faceless characters that sit on Football Association committees – and decided that they must be held to account for their decisions, one of which had been to dock the Teesside club three points, indirectly precipitating their demotion, for failing to fulfil a fixture against Blackburn Rovers because of an epidemic of injury and illness.

After several weeks of First Division football, Mr Arnott could stand it no more and issued a claim against the FA for the "loss of enjoyment" that the absence of top-flight fare at the Riverside was causing him. Arguing that the governing body's guidelines on unfulfilled fixtures were unclear, he took the FA to the small claims court to try to recover the £342 cost of his season ticket.

Terrace Terror

1/10

The court ruled that Mr Arnott had not been forced to purchase his season ticket and therefore the organisation had no duty of care, but there had been concerns that defeat for the FA in this test case would have resulted in 26,000 other Teessiders turning up at Soho Square, letters from Claims Direct in their grasping fingers.

5

The Burnley Few

February 1996

I t can't be easy being a footballer's wife: for all the Gucci handbags, designer clothes, five-bedroom mock-Tudor mansions and six-figure divorce settlements, there is a price to be paid, if not in the shape of a busty model prepared to daub her husband's carnal preferences all over the front of the *News of the World*, then in the form of the general disparagement of the wider public (readers of *Hello* excepted).

Yet there is one other peripheral character in the football narrative whose plaintive voice is rarely heard: the manager's wife. If she's not having to survey the detritus of her husband's Saturday evening post-defeat strops, she's probably putting up with threatening phone calls in the middle of the night.

But worst of all must be the treatment reserved for the wife of Jimmy Mullen by a group of Burnley fans, after he had followed the club's promotion to Division One in 1994 with relegation 12 months later and a rotten pre-Christmas spell in the next campaign. Spotting her trying to grab a consolation fish supper in one of the town's chip shops, one of them snuck out a cigarette lighter and allegedly tried to set her dress on fire.

Terrace Terror

7/10

Madness, with a capital M. Fortunately, Mrs Mullen proved not to be highly flammable, but the incident was witnessed by the manager and their son as they sat outside in the car and was enough to persuade him that the disadvantages of remaining in charge at Turf Moor were beginning to outweigh the benefits. Although Mullen claimed that reports of the incident were sensationalised – Burnley police would confirm only that a lighter was involved, not that it was used to set fire to anyone – by the end of the week, he was gone.

6

Sabaean Myers
Burnley v Preston
Division One. Turf Moor. March 2002

It is hard to know how to mark the arrival of genius in your native land, but it is probably true to say that Sebaean Myers' "cheeky celebration", as one newspaper described it, of Paul Gascoigne's inauguration into Burnley colours would have been fully appreciated by the arch-clown himself. With Burnley 2–0 up in this Lancashire derby, Myers, a 20-year-old builder's labourer, decided to get up close and personal with the opposing supporters. Stripping off his civvies and whipping out a particularly impressive marker pen, Myers persuaded a mate to scribble the scoreline on his backside (one figure per buttock) before leaping from the crowd and running to the goal behind which the Preston fans were amassed. There, he turned, bent over and pointed to the faint but indelible imprint on his gluteus maximus, leaving them with an unmistakeable image to accompany them on the journey back to Deepdale.

That might have been sufficient farce to lace the afternoon's entertainment for most of the Burnley faithful, but there was more to come, in the form of another club legend – Bertie the Bee, the Turf Moor mascot. While stewards and police fumbled and faltered in their efforts to apprehend the intruder, Bertie launched a sting operation, luring Myers into his honey-trap before rudely upending him.

Terrace Terror

2/10

Barely annoying. Myers' antics landed him in front of magistrates, *where he avoided a football banning order after telling the court he was actually a Liverpool supporter who thought the game had needed livening up. Bertie, meanwhile, remained modest about his intervention in the incident. "Me and Bumble often pretend to fight when we're in the hive," he told one incredulous journalist. "Carrying pollen around all day makes you strong and he was just a featherweight, so I flipped him over my shoulder and pinned him down. It was a good move and one I've seen on the WWF before."*

7

Unnamed Dunstable Town fan
Dunstable Town v AFC Wimbledon
FA Cup second qualifying round.
Creasey Park Stadium. October 2004

There was widespread derision among the 1,700-strong band of travelling AFC Wimbledon supporters when, with his team trailing 3-0 and 20 minutes still remaining, the announcer on the Dunstable Town PA system named Paul Taylor, the home team's goalkeeper, as the sponsors' man of the match.

The visiting fans were entitled to think the accolade should have gone to their midfield maestro Rob Ursell, who had scored the most skilful of hat-tricks to put the game beyond doubt. One Dunstable follower, however, was so overwhelmed with the need to congratulate the award winner that he stripped naked and ran the length of the pitch to jump into the goalkeeper's arms. That he then slid in from behind to up-end one of the referee's assistants endeared him less to his fellow Dunstable supporters, who had worked tirelessly to tidy up the Southern League club's ground for their biggest match since George Best had played for them in a pre-season friendly in the early 1970s. It did, though, give one spectator the

chance to observe that the miscreant had produced the best tackle he had seen all afternoon.

Terrace Terror
6/10

It later emerged that the man, known to home officials only as Moggsy, was a bit of a serial stripper, who had treated the Bedfordshire town to the sight of his todger on more than one previous occasion.

8

Terry Jamieson
Newport Isle of Wight.

Isthmian League. St George's Park. June 1991

The Isle of Wight is truly a happening place. Within a matter of weeks, its main paper, the *County Press*, was first with the story about a 57-year-old tortoise that had gone missing – the bid for freedom was shortlived when it was found several days later wandering along the road a few yards from his home; was first on the scene when the visit to the island of David Icke, the former Coventry City goalkeeper-cum-Son of God – a personal saver turned personal saviour, if you like – caused gridlock at the ferry terminal; and got the exclusive on a man being barred from the ground of its leading non-league football team.

But this was no ordinary man: it was Terry Jamieson, the governor of Her Majesty's Prison, Albany, someone more used to doing the locking in than being locked out. Jamieson was outraged to receive a letter from the club's committee telling him that his behaviour at games had, like one of Icke's theories, "transcended the acceptable". While admitting that his heckling had never been obscene, secretary Chris Cheverton complained that his comments were of "a sniping nature, personal and often aimed at the manager, the chairman, or," – and here he paused to dab his eyes with his handkerchief – "me."

Terrace Terror

3/10

Ridiculously unscary. Jamieson, a cousin of one of the club's former managers, branded their action "silly", suggesting the team could hardly expect unbridled praise when they hadn't scored for seven games.

9

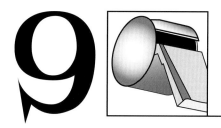

Queens Park mob
Queens Park v Preston North End
October 1886

Pasuckualohowog is not a word you're likely to hear on your average edition of *Countdown*, even the numerically gifted Carol Vorderman being hard-pressed to come up with the requisite amount of vowels and consonants to satisfy such a sequence of syllables. More than 1,000 people at a time took part in the fun of this Native American form of the beautiful game, on a field half a mile wide and with goals a mile apart. The contests, history reports, were often rough, resulting in many a broken bone, not to mention head-dress, yet retribution on the transgressor was rare for the simple reason that the ornaments and war paint they wore prevented easy identification. It is unlikely that officials of Scottish club Queens Park were aware of the goings-on at the settlements, but they found a similar approach handy after James Ross, the Preston North End inside-left, had surreptitiously knocked out a Queens Park defender in retaliation for a hack from behind during the Lancashire club's victory in this early FA Cup encounter. As an unruly mob of home fans swarmed towards the changing rooms in an attempt to get their hands on the unfortunate Ross, the officials disguised him and smuggled him to the waiting train.

Terrace Terror

8/10

The hairy Highland hordes were seldom as scary again until they tried to raze and rebuild Wembley after victory in the home international of 1977. Ross survived to take his place in FA Cup history by scoring eight goals in the record 26-0 win over Hyde in the first round a year later, safe from the vengeance of the Queen's Park faithful after the club, twice runners-up to Blackburn in the English version, decided to concentrate on the Scottish version of the competition.

All football clubs attract their eccentrics and, mostly, they're fairly harmless. Take Jimmy Jump, of Barcelona, for example: the self-styled "human football" ran on to the pitch at the final of Euro 2004, swerved past Luis Figo and hurled himself into the back of the Portugal net, an art he performs, according to his website, in the name of "amusement and liberty", although he usually finds himself in the back of a police van before you've stopped laughing. Fleeting though it may be, his contribution to the sport is obvious. But, try as you might, it is hard to appreciate what Joe Radio, a fan of the second division Sport Club de Recife in Brazil, brings to the game. Well, actually, what he brings to the game is a heavy antique wireless, which he uses to debilitating effect on the opposition. Radio's proud boast is that although he attends each of his team's games, he never actually watches them. Instead, he takes up a position close to the away team's dugout, with his back to the action, from where he hurls abuse at the visiting manager and substitutes. When momentarily lost for expletives, he turns up the volume on his primeval ghetto-blaster and aims its cacophonous din in their direction to put them off their game.

Terrace Terror

6/10

Frightening. A former military policeman, Radio displays a discomforting knowledge of the average South American dictatorship's methods of torture. But the moustachioed former soldier insists there is nothing sinister in his behaviour, claiming that he originally took the radio along to listen to the commentary and only gradually observed the disquieting effects it could have on rivals.

Andrew Jane
Tranmere Rovers v Oxford United
Division Two. Prenton Park. May 1992

Far out in the supporting hinterland lives a strange and much misunderstood creature, an animal that, unlike most of the species, rarely hunts in a pack, preferring the kind of solitary pleasures that only possession of an enormous bundle of broadsheet newspapers, a return rail ticket to Carlisle or Torquay, and the absence of anything else remotely resembling a life, can confer – one in whom, in short, the love for the game substantially outweighs an allegiance to one club. It is known as: the would-be member of the 92 Club, an exclusive band of fans who have visited all the English league grounds.

One example of the breed was Andrew Jane, nominally an Oxford United supporter, who decided to take advantage of the fact that his club's final game of the 1991-2 season was at Prenton Park, by coincidence the only ground that had failed to host this happiest of wanderers. When the home club was told of his intention to attend, they honoured him with a mention in the match programme. Unfortunately, Jane never got to read the warm Wirral welcome, his celebrations of his achievement with his fellow fans resulting in him being arrested for drunkenness on his way to the stadium.

Terrace Terror

2/10

Hardly. Jane was fined 50 quid when he made an appearance at one venue that had not been on his list: Wirral magistrates court.

12 Unused substitute

Sportsmanship is a rare and declining commodity these days. While clubs make all the right noises, condemning the abusive and playing lip service to a supposed desire for fair play, the truth of the matter is that they really wouldn't have it any other way. The veracity of this statement was made clear in a manner of some brutality to one Real Madrid supporter who, one morning as long ago as 1961, found himself confronted by some quite unwelcome correspondence on his doormat. It was a letter from the club informing him that he was to be banned from the stadium for nine months and fined a whopping £3. The abominable crime he had committed that required such an extreme sanction? He had been spotted applauding when the opposition scored. And this from a club that had published a club history earlier the same year in which the authors complained that "in the face of much hostility on away grounds, Real have played silently, with sportsmanship and with something akin to nobility". Nonetheless the bemused supporter, informed that he "must not encourage our opponents", had to go to court to get the suspension overturned.

Chapter Eight

The worst
goalkeeping
errors

Worst goalkeeping errors

Tom Farquharson, a Cardiff City goalkeeper of the 1920s, had a habit that would have given any penalty-taker greater pause for thought than whether to put the ball left, right or straight down the middle: he often kept a handgun in a bag in the back of the net. Welsh international Leigh Richmond Roose, a man of independent means from a slightly earlier era, chose to neglect his doctorate in bacteriology for a career between the posts for Stoke, Everton, Stoke again, Sunderland, Port Vale, Huddersfield and Aston Villa, regularly chartering a personal train to steam him to the required venue from his home in London. John Burridge, meanwhile, used to scare the bedsocks off his wife in the many homes they inhabited during his 15-club career by conducting interviews with the likes of John Motson and Gerald Sinstadt in his sleep. If you sense a theme developing here, you'd be right, and it's the age-old one about goalkeepers being a breed apart. But since the game's early days, when those occupying the position were referred to as stiffies, Victorian slang for unskilled labourers, or funk-sticks, a term implying cowardice, that notion of "standing out" has assumed a more positive connotation. But if goalkeepers are proud to accept their improved status, and expect to be lauded when they show their worth, they can pay a high price for being the one true individual in a team game – and that's a price involving severe personal humiliation, as the examples to come show. (NB: Aston Villa fans may be advised to look away now.)

1

Peter Enckelman
Birmingham City v Aston Villa
The Premiership. St Andrews.
September 2002

Among the main attributes a goalkeeper requires are courage, concentration, speed of thought, determination, and, as one humorist pointed out, an IQ of under 20. Peter Enckelman had the first four qualities in abundance, but when he allowed a throw-in from team-mate Olof Mellberg to briefly brush his foot before continuing its natural progress into the back of his own net – giving Villa's second-city rivals a two-goal lead in the 77th minute – it was suggested he was in possession of the fifth, particularly by Graham Taylor, the Villa manager, who accused the Finn of not knowing the rules. Had the goalkeeper allowed the ball from the throw-in to run directly into goal untouched, it would not have counted – a corner would have been given.

Along with his manager's ire, Enckelman had to put up with the provocation of a beered-up Bluenose fan who, not content with appreciating the goalkeeper's discomfort from the sidelines like his fellow supporters and the millions around the world watching the match live on TV, felt compelled to run on to the pitch and laugh in his face.

Saving Grace

8/10

The tabloids went into a *frenzy the next morning, billing it as "the most bizarre goalkeeping blunder in history". Perhaps it was, to those whose familiarity with football started with the purchase of a Sky TV digibox, but further research reveals a much more common malaise. The next night, Kelvin Davis committed a near carbon-copy of Enckelman's error for Wimbledon against Portsmouth, and before the month was out, two more members of the goalkeepers' union, Phil Barnes of Blackpool, and 17-year-old third-choice stopper Stuart Robertson, of Queen of the South, had been tarred with the Enckelman brush.*

2

Amongst those Villa supporters who know their history, even Enckelman's idiocy has not managed to erase from their consciousness the name of an equally talented, but flawed, custodian. Cyril Spiers may have committed his gaffe more than 80 years ago, and been dead for nearly 40, but his howler in the first second-city derby of the 1925-26 season lives on. Villa led 3-0 with eleven minutes left, and some Birmingham supporters sloped off to catch an early bus home, though Victor Milne, the qualified doctor who attended to the health of the Villa midfield, went down injured and was forced to limp ineffectively through the remainder of the match on the left wing. As Villa tried to come to terms with the positional reorganisation this required, Joe Bradford, who'd once had trials at Villa Park, extracted a measure of vengeance on those who had rejected him, taking advantage of a miskick to make it 3-1. Two minutes later, the Birmingham centre-forward struck again, and the home crowd grew a little restless. But there was worse to follow as, almost immediately, Spiers went down to gather a harmless long shot, slipped, and in trying to push the ball out, managed only to throw it into his own net.

Saving Grace

6/10

Villa Park was built on the site of a Victorian amusement park, so maybe the mischievous ghosts of that era were working some sinister alchemy to bring out the clown in Spiers. It was certainly enough to lower the spirits of the usually reliable goalkeeper, whose Villa career went downhill thereafter, with an injury that followed later that season leading to his release.

3

Peter Schmeichel
Aston Villa v Liverpool
The Premiership, Villa Park, December 2000

Reminiscent of an over-zealous head of security at a shopping centre, Peter Schmeichel was given to patrolling his area and handing out admonishments to anyone who started mucking about on his watch. Yet, on those rare occasions when he was the one to indulge in a bit of work-hour horseplay, such was the force of his personality that few dared to pin the blame on him for any unwelcome fallout; those who did were usually the recipients of a few choice words in a mixture of Danish and Manc that left them with the notion that the fault was theirs all along. So, when one of his long-distance throw-outs hit referee Andy D'Urso on the back and Jari Litmanen stroked the rebounding ball into the unguarded net, Schmeichel was met not with a group of team-mates on his case, braying at him for leaving his goal vulnerable to attack, but by complete silence – which, in its way, got their message across even more effectively. This time, even Schmeichel was wise enough not to go looking for a scape-goat, although when he subsequently hurled another off-target throw directly into touch, he turned on any player within range and blasted them for his mistake.

Saving Grace

6/10

The seventh-minute goal proved crucial in Liverpool's 2-1 win, but even Villa manager John Gregory was too scared of the great Dane to suggest that he was at fault. Instead, he turned his sarcasm on D'Urso. "I don't blame the keeper at all," he said. "You don't expect the ref to get in the way like that. He showed great skill to bring the ball down, then shouted at Litmanen to go on and score. But it was a bit strong when he ran down to the Liverpool end to celebrate."

Bob Anderson
Arsenal v Middlesbrough
Division One. Highbury. March 1948

According to recent research, a certain amount of stress in the workplace is a positive thing, helping to keep a person focused, energised and able to perform better. Goalkeepers disagree. Such was the horror of Bob Anderson's showing on his debut in goal for Middlesbrough, for instance, that not even a warehouse-full of Chesterfields piled up around the edge of the Highbury pitch could have saved him from exposure to the critical eyes of a 60,000 crowd. The first gaffe came after only five minutes, the 23-year-old misjudging the flight of Don Roper's looping shot from the wing, and after Denis Compton had added the second and Ron Rooke the third, Anderson gifted them the fourth. Dicky Robinson's wild clearance soared into the air and, blinded by the sun, the unfortunate stopper lunged a second too late and turned to find the ball nestling in the net. Compton grabbed the fifth before Anderson faltered again, and most eccentrically, failing to get any lift from his goal-kick, which hit a surprised Rooke on the back and rebounded back over the goalkeeper for number six. He was only partly implicated in the seventh and final goal, failing to reach George Hardwick's short back-pass and Rooke intercepted to complete his hat-trick.

Saving Grace
7/10

Good Friday it may have been, but not for Anderson, who was dropped for the next game at Maine Road and the Easter Monday return against Arsenal. And the match after that. In fact, he was not selected for the next four years and was transferred, that one appearance to his name, to Crystal Palace. It was a strange recurring pattern for the Anderson family; younger brother William had made his debut in goal for Newcastle a year earlier – and never got another game at professional level.

Barry Roche
Derby County v Nottingham Forest
Division One, Pride Park, March 2004

It is rare for an individual fan to have a direct impact on proceedings on the pitch, but the supporter who discarded the coffee cup – the reports were adamant that it was not tea, or Bovril – that drifted over the touchline and was blown towards the edge of Barry Roche's penalty area by winds that had buffeted Forest followers travelling the A52 from Nottingham to Derby, would have been, depending on his allegiance, cursing or congratulating himself on not using the bin. For although Derby had taken a third-minute lead through Ian Taylor, it was shortly before the half-hour that the game turned significantly their way. Wes Morgan played a routine back-pass towards the left edge of Roche's area, and as the Forest goalkeeper set himself to hoof upfield, the rogue beaker breezed into its final, and fateful, position, right in the line of the ball. Roche swung his right foot, but failed to account for the bobble the ball took from the beverage container, skewed his clearance, and allowed Paul Peschisolido to turn and volley into an empty net.

Saving Grace
6/10

Peschosolido, who nabbed another one later and set up Marcus Tudgay's fourth, admitted to some sympathy for Roche. "I felt sorry for the 'keeper," he said. "I was about to turn round when it bounced off his shin. I thought, 'here we go, it's Christmas'." Roche, whose mistake had cost his side two points in their previous match against Burnley, suggested defiantly he would recover from the ignominy, but with Derby's win taking them to within a point of their relegation rivals, no-one was entirely convinced.

6

Dan Lewis
Cardiff City v Arsenal
FA Cup final, Wembley, April 1927

Dan Lewis played 142 games for Arsenal between 1924 and 1929, but it is one appearance in his spell at Highbury by which he is defined. Indeed, look for his name in almost any history book and you will find each and every reference to him accompanied by the words that must have haunted him up until his death in 1965: FA Cup final, Wembley, 1927. For it is in this match that the Welshman, playing for the English team, let a harmless shot from a Scotsman, playing for the Welsh side, to creep over his line and allowed the trophy to be taken out of its home country for the first time. It was in the 74th minute of a frankly disappointing goalless game that Hugh Ferguson acquired the ball from a throw-in and advanced on the Arsenal goal. The prolific striker, Motherwell born and bred, fired in a reasonable, but not venomous, effort from about 20 yards that Lewis, in normal circumstances, would have been expected to deal with without undue alarm. But this time, as he went down to save it, panic seemed to take over, and he produced a series of limb actions that suggested he was being controlled by a giant, invisible and somewhat inept puppeteer – or perhaps that he'd suddenly acquired a plastic pole up his backside, like a prototype Subbuteo goalie. Having seemingly stopped the ball, his subsequent involuntary movements sent the ball trickling towards the goal – and as a BBC radio presenter, broadcasting commentary from a final for the first time, found his Queen's English hard to force from out the back of his larynx, it inched over the line for the only score of the game.

Saving Grace
9/10

Lewis was so gutted that after the presentations he hurled his losers' medal to the turf and stormed away. Team-mate Bob John retrieved it, however, and tried to console Lewis with the words: "Forget it Dan, there'll be another chance." There was, for Arsenal, when they returned to Wembley three years later to face Huddersfield Town – but Lewis got injured a week before the final. Later the error was blamed on Lewis's shiny new jersey, and the legend developed that all subsequent Arsenal Cup Final goalkeepers had to wear a shirt that had been worn or washed.

7

Ray Clemence
Scotland v England
Home Internationals, Hampden Park,
May 1976

Bill Shankly had had Ray Clemence watched several times before signing him from Scunthorpe, completing his rise from Skegness beach attendant to First Division goalkeeper, but it was the rare combination of being a strong left-foot kicker who was nonetheless good on his right-hand side that finally convinced the Liverpool manager that he was something special. England never had cause to question his ability on either flank, but they were left to wonder about his capability of dealing with a ball struck straight at him when Kenny Dalglish, just weeks before becoming Clemence's Liverpool team-mate, oozed a total miskick between the goalkeeper's legs at Hampden Park to give Scotland a 2-1 victory. Some admirers of the goalkeeper sought to find mitigation in the fact that Clemence had been fooled because he was anticipating a powerful drive from the striker, but the combination of the painful lack of pace in the 49th-minute shot and the agonisingly ungainly manner in which Clemence attempted to save – like a new-born fawn unable to stay on its feet – only added to the embarrassment.

Saving Grace

8/10

When reminded of the error, Clemence has the perfect riposte in the form of winners' medals from five league championships and three European Cups. Yet one historian has referred to it as "the skeleton in Clemence's cupboard" and the goalkeeper himself has described it as the worst moment of his career. "I thought I had the ball covered," he said, "but it bobbled and the next thing I knew it was through my legs and in the net. I wanted the pitch to open up and hide me."

8

Ian Walker
Leicester City v Bolton Wanderers
The Premiership. Walkers Stadium.
February 2004

Tom Bushnell was a self-taught psychologist who had learnt to break planks of wood with his bare hands; Ian Walker was a goalkeeper who had forgotten how to catch leather with his. The two were brought together when Bushnell demonstrated his talent – otherwise only useful when he'd got locked out at night – to the Leicester City players, 11 games without a victory, to stress the importance of mind over matter. Having promised Foxes manager Micky Adams that a session with him was certain to secure three points, Leicester started in fine style against high-flying Bolton, Les Ferdinand giving them an early lead. But whatever positive thoughts Bushnell had implanted in Walker's head were no match for the sorcery of Sam Allardyce, who took advantage of new guidelines on offside to stir up a ferment of uncertainty in the City goalkeeper's thinking. The Bolton boss planted two players in apparent offside positions on either corner of Walker's six-yard box, the pair running away from goal to avoid an infringement as Youri Djorkaeff chipped in a free kick from ten yards outside the penalty area. Kevin Davies, running in with defenders as the ball was delivered, got the merest of touches in front of Walker, yet it was hardly enough to beat a man capped by his country, who seemed to safely gather the ball just in front of his body. Yet frame-by-frame video analysis no doubt undertaken by Adams before training the next morning would prove this to be only partly the case. The ball had slipped slightly from the goalkeeper's grasp, and in hastily trying to grab it before Davies could launch any follow-up, Walker succeeded only in slipping it under his body, where his trailing leg applied the finishing touch.

Saving Grace

7/10

Allardyce's interpretation of the new guidelines, handed out by FIFA and passed on to referees but which seemed to have eluded television pundits, most of the paying public and a good number of club managers, caused a furore among bureaucrats, who met to try to counter the tactic. From that meeting it was ordered that a player considered to be 'deceiving or distracting' while in an offside position should be flagged. It was of little comfort to Walker: heaped on top of his shame was the news that the Bolton equaliser had been registered as an own goal.

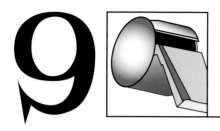

Jerzy Dudek
Liverpool v Manchester United
The Premiership. Anfield. December 2002

According to South American writer Eduardo Galeano, the goalkeeper is football's wet blanket, snuffing out, as he generally does, the lifeblood of the game: goals. Yet within a month of signing a new four-year contract at Anfield, Jerzy Dudek could have hung a damp continental quilt from his crossbar and piled dripping duck-down pillows behind him in the six-yard area and still found himself unable to keep the opposition from scoring. Errors against Middlesbrough, Basle and Fulham were bad enough, but Galeano's Uruguayan compatriot Diego Forlan benefited most from his loss of form. It seemed the easiest of tasks for Dudek to bend down and gather Jamie Carragher's headed back-pass in the 64th minute, but Carragher, and about 40,000 other

Scousers, were left to watch in mounting horror as Dudek allowed it to slip through his hands and legs, and Forlan ran in to tap home. Three minutes later, the striker took advantage of his renewed confidence to shoot towards the near post, where the Pole again allowed the ball to escape his grasp. Liverpool boss Gerard Houllier was so shocked by the resulting 2-1 defeat that, afterwards, he offered a blatheringly inadequate explanation. "If Jerzy hadn't let in the first," he said, "I don't think he'd have conceded the second."

Saving Grace

6/10

Critics traced Dudek's difficulties back to the previous summer's World Cup finals, pointing to errors made in the Far East against South Korea and Portugal as prompting his decline. The Pole was inclined to agree, moaning that the competition took him to "the limit" of his physical powers. "The tournament made a big impression on me," he said, "and because the English fixture calendar is overloaded I was unable to recover from it. I need a period of rest." Houllier concurred, and promptly dropped him.

Steve Cherry
Derby County v Chelsea
Division Two. The Baseball Ground.
January 1984

Positioning is everything for a goalkeeper, although there are few funnier sights than one who pulls off an athletic, full-length save to a shot that everyone watching knows is going several feet wide. Better save than sorry, as it were – but Derby's Steve Cherry made a spectacular save, and ended up deeply sorry. When Dave Watson, the Derby defender, tried to show the class that brought him 65 England caps by volleying a misdirected cross-field ball from the middle of his own half back to Steve Cherry, the Chelsea fans behind the goal were delighted to see that the ball was sailing way off target, and began to savour the forthcoming corner that would give them a chance to break the deadlock. Cherry, however, could sense only that the ball was floating over his head intent on nestling in the back of his net. Starting to back-pedal furiously, he finally caught up with it sufficiently to execute a spectacular salmon-like backwards leap and make significant contact. When he landed, he found himself not in the centre of his goal, his team-mates ready to give him a hand up and congratulate him on his athleticism, but a good three feet outside his nearest post and the ball dribbling over his goal line.

Saving Grace

6/10

In a truly selfless act, Cherry rescued his more illustrious team-mate from widespread ridicule, heaping instead the scorn of Baseball Ground regulars upon his own, no doubt sagging, shoulders. But what did he get for his troubles? A transfer to Third Division Walsall, that's what, where he was to come up against his relegated team-mates the following year, while Chelsea went on to win 2-1 and snatch the Second Division title from Sheffield Wednesday on goal difference.

11

Frank Haffey
England v Scotland
Home International, Wembley Stadium, 1961

The Celtic goalkeeper, perennially Scotland's second- or third-choice custodian, let in nine goals against England at Wembley in April 1961 on his second – and last – international appearance, but he was happily warbling away in the bath until Denis Law pointed out to him that he had been responsible for Scottish football's worst catastrophe. Haffey didn't take it to heart, and while his team-mates ducked beneath window level as their coach passed unhappy hordes of their own supporters on the drive back down Wembley Way, Haffey smiled and waved at the tartan-clad troops (although another report suggests he had to hide in a nearby house until they had dispersed). He was even more accommodating when the team arrived at King's

Cross for the rail journey home, allowing his grinning face to be photographed beneath the sign for platform nine, a picture that would be staring out from the first editions by the time the train had reached Glasgow. But while the papers were keen to blame Haffey for the disaster, the truth is that few reports could highlight for which of the goals he had been culpable, and members of England's line-up, one of the country's finest of all time, believed they would have run amok whoever had been in goal.

Saving Grace
9/10

Haffey, a man who would climb onto his own crossbar and pretend to fall asleep when the action was up the opposite end, always seemed to save his worst for the big occasion. Two weeks after the Wembley debacle, he dropped a simple shot from Charlie Dickson, after a Dunfermline breakaway three minutes from the end, to confirm the Pars' first Scottish Cup win. Eleven months later, a similar blunder against Airdrie derailed Celtic's pursuit of Dundee and Rangers for the league title.

Unused substitute

he Honourable Arthur Kinnaird, an aristocratic gentleman of leisure of the type that dominated the game in its early years, was such a hero that on arrival at Kennington Oval for the 1877 FA Cup final, where he was to represent the Wanderers against Oxford University, he had hardly disembarked from his coach and horses before he was hoisted up on to the shoulders of supporters and carried all the way to the dressing-room entrance. Sadly, the Scotsman, notable for a luxuriant long ginger beard and a palatial estate in Perthshire, had to make his own way back to his transport later that afternoon after dropping an almighty clanger that could have cost his team the spoils. It might be fair to say that Kinnaird spread his talents widely –

of the nine finals he played in, six were in Old Etonians' colours – and while primarily an outfield player, he did hog the limelight by performing handstands on the pitch and sometimes going in goal. That was to prove his undoing in this match, when, with the score still 0-0, he caught a cross and inadvertently stepped back across the goal-line with ball in hand. It was the first own goal in FA Cup final history, yet for a century Kinnaird's guilt was hidden from the world: the University's strike was somehow lost in contemporary reports of the game and only unearthed by eagle-eyed statisticians many moons later. Fortunately for Kinnaird, his team-mates scored twice to clinch the trophy.

The worst sendings off

The worst sendings off

Self-righteous commentators will tell you that "it spoiled the game as a contest" or "nobody likes to see this sort of thing", but it is a fact that the dismissal of a footballer from the field of play is, like a goal or a controversial penalty, one of the dramatic high-points of a game. There are few things that the average crowd enjoys more than the opportunity to launch into a rousing chorus of "off, off, off", especially when the miscreant is one of the more hated members of the opposition and their own player has managed to convince the official that the merest nudge in the back has left him in need of months of reconstructive surgery. Even referees themselves, though they will deny it, can be seen to experience a small shiver of anticipation in the moment they realise they have the opportunity to assert their ultimate authority. Take Jack Taylor. One of the most esteemed referees of the past half-century, renowned for his diplomatic skills when the pressure was on, even he was forced to admit in his autobiography that he kept "a few clippings in a scrapbook" of the men he had sent for an early bath, while David Elleray, everyone's favourite Harrow house-master, has owned up to secreting away some records of his most notorious expulsions. So let us have no more of this sanctimony and, instead, take time to appreciate the sending off in all its awful, but multi-faceted, glory.

1

Ambrose Brown
Hull City v Wrexham
Division Three North. Boothferry Park.
December 1936

Christmas Day 1936 was not a good day for shipping, as the Hull Daily Mail was quick to point out; one vessel that was a regular visitor to the local docks was disabled as it left Mauritius, a second lost 20 passengers to a boiler explosion on the way out of Eritrea and a third got trapped on mudbanks just outside Southampton. When Ambrose Brown, an inside left for Wrexham, got sent off with less than a minute on the clock of this festive fixture at Boothferry Park, his team-mates must have felt they, too, had been holed below the water line before they'd made it out of the harbour. The precise timing of the incident remains a mystery known only to the referee and his pocket watch – some say as few as 20 seconds of the match had elapsed – but suffice to say that Brown, marked out as the villain of an aerial clash of elbows with City left half Jim Treanor that left both writhing on the ground, was back in North Wales in time to finish off the turkey sandwiches.

Not that this was the only instance of Brown, signed after a successful season with Chesterfield, showing his familiarity with the geography of trouble: some weeks later, after an FA Cup match against Manchester City, he was one of four team members charged with "imbibing intoxicating liquor in non-permitted hours" at a town centre inn after being unable to adequately account to a local constable for an incriminating half of shandy positioned in front of him on the bar.

Early Bath Temperature

4/10

Still cold. Fined ten shillings by Wrexham magistrates for the drinking violation, there is no note of any measures taken against Brown for the dismissal. Nevertheless, the forward, who made 27 appearances for Wrexham that season, was shipped out of the Racecourse Ground at the end of the campaign, his brief career sinking without trace in the outposts of Bath City and Tunbridge Wells Rangers.

Nobby Stiles
Estudiantes v Man Utd
World Club Championship.
Boca Juniors Stadium. September 1968

Manchester United may have gone to Argentina as European champions, but in a stadium nicknamed 'The Chocolate Box' because of its steeply-stacked surrounds, the welcome was anything but sweet. Nobby Stiles knew he was in trouble as soon as he stepped blinking into the light of the arrivals lounge at Buenos Aires airport. While George Best was being greeted with a banner proclaiming him, with slightly iffy geography, El Beatle, Bobby Charlton was being lauded as The Champion, and Denis Law trumpeted as The King, Stiles was made the focal point for the ill-feeling left over from the fractious England-Argentina World Cup quarter-final two years earlier, and dismissed as The Bandit. Any signs of lawlessness, however, came from the South American champions: when a United player leapt for a corner, he would feel not the satisfying contact of forehead on leather, but increasingly large globules of Argentinian spittle; when a United player fell, an opponent would help him up in an apparent spirit of conciliation – by the hairs of his armpit. Stiles tried to give as good as he was getting, and when Carlos Bilardo, later a very successful national team coach, went face to face with him, the pair exchanged headbutts. But the little defender's greatest troubles were reserved for the second half, when he was hauled up for offside after being put through by Paddy Crerand. Senor Sosa Miranda, the Paraguayan referee, was not too happy when Stiles observed through the alarming gap in his teeth that the official must be blind, and asked the diminutive Mancunian for verification of his accusation. When Stiles noted that he must be "f***ing deaf as well", it was, perhaps not surprisingly, the final opinion of any sort he was allowed to voice on proceedings.

Early Bath Temperature

7/10

Steaming. Stiles could hardly believe he had been dismissed for dissent while his comrades were being felled all about him. However, he and his team-mates were just glad to get out alive, and with the chance to return the hospitality when Estudiantes, leading 1–0 from the first leg, travelled to Old Trafford for the return. Yet, once in Manchester, the Argentinians continued the dirty tricks campaign, escaping with the silverware as Best this time fell victim, sent off after lashing out at Medina following a crude challenge.

3

Andy Morrison
Fulham v Manchester City
Division One. Craven Cottage.
August 1999

Q **: What's the definition of disgust?**
A: When your granny gives you a birthday
kiss and slips her tongue in.

It's an old joke and, while usually able to elicit a
laugh from a teenage boy, it would probably not
be fully appreciated by Stan Collymore who, in an
otherwise uneventful goalless draw, was forced
to play the adolescent to Andy Morrison's elderly
relative. Taking too literally the advice of referee
Paul Rejer to kiss and make up after the pair had
rounded on each other following an aerial clash,
Morrison initiated a move that, had it taken place
with a stranger in a car park, would probably not
have bothered Collymore overmuch. As it was,
the Aston Villa striker, at the time on loan to

Fulham, did not welcome such intimate attention. Rejer wasn't overly impressed either, interrupting the impromptu clinch by waving a yellow card the way of the hulking City centre-back. It was only when the crowd started baying that Rejer realised that that was not the end of the matter, for he had earlier cautioned Morrison for upending Geoff Horsfield, and he was left with no option but to produce the red – in so doing becoming the first official to dismiss a player for an unsolicited on-field snog.

Early Bath Temperature

5/10

Turn down the thermostat.

Collymore dampened any hopes Morrison might have had for a longer-term relationship when he dismissed the defender in his autobiography as a "journeyman squaddie". Joe Royle, the City manager, was equally unhappy, but in his case with the official. "When are referees going to realise it's a man's game and sometimes gets physical," he roared, seemingly without a hint of irony.

Nigel Pepper

Darlington v York City. Division Four. Feethams.
September 1990: Darlington v York City. FA Cup first
round. Feethams. November 1990: York City v Darlington.
Division Four. Bootham Crescent. February 1991

When he arrived at Aberdeen from Bradford City in 1998, Nigel Pepper, a midfielder hewn from the hardest rock, would have seemed the perfect man to stoke the engine room for the team from the Granite City – and, as an Englishman, at least cause a rethink of Scottish stereotypes about soft southerners. Four sendings-off in a harrowing year – one of them just six minutes after coming on as a sub against Celtic, and another, against Dundee United on his return from suspension, after only 15 seconds – saw him dispatched back over Hadrian's Wall. Storming examples of the sending-off art that these undoubtedly are, they do not do complete justice to a master exponent. For some years earlier, when with his second club York City, he was to prove that, whatever you do, some teams will always bring out the worst in you. For Pepper, one of those teams was Darlington. In four games in one season against the Cleveland club – two in the league and two in the cup – he managed to remain on the pitch until the end in only one, although, according to those that were there, his straight red in the 89th minute of the last, at Feetham's in February, was highly contentious.

Early Bath Temperature

 7/10

Spicy. Pepper was remarkably sanguine about his bad-boy reputation: "The refs make decisions and when you get sent off you often think they are the wrong ones," he once said, although on arriving at Scunthorpe, his sixth club, in 2000, he showed that time had not dulled his senses: laid out on the ground with a double fracture of his leg after a challenge by Paul Webb, of Kidderminster Harriers, he still had enough about him to lamp the perpetrator; as he was carried off the referee brandished the inevitable red card.

5

Walter Boyd
Swansea City v Darlington
Division Three. The Vetch Field.
November 1999

Cradling his best friend after he had been shot by gangsters in their home town of Kingston, Jamaica, Walter Boyd showed remarkable self-possession when the killers drove up to him and asked: "Do you have a problem with that?" "No man, no problem," Boyd wisely replied, and the gunmen screeched away, leaving the striker - known as "the black Gazza" for his unusual bag of tricks – unharmed, and his mate to breathe his last in his arms. Dramatic story as it is, it serves a purpose in illustrating that Boyd was hardly the kind of man you would expect to lose it in a pressure situation. But the savage winds of South Wales can do strange things to someone more used to the bountiful breezes and abundant sunshine of the Caribbean and, brought on as a late substitute against Darlington, he took umbrage at a spot of pushing and tugging on the edge of the visitors' box by Martin Gray, and flattened the Quakers midfielder before referee Clive Wilkes had had a chance to restart the game. Given a straight red, it was later confirmed that the international had made history by becoming the first player to be sent off after zero seconds.

Early Bath Temperature

 8/10

Heated. Gray afterwards denied he had used any racist language to wind up the Jamaican, saying that there was merely a bit of argy-bargy before Boyd "whacked him on the side of the face". Boyd escaped any immediate censure from Swansea boss John Hollins, but was later left out of the team when he turned up late for a meeting.

6

Billy Bremner and Kevin Keegan
Leeds United v Liverpool
Charity Shield, Wembley, August 1974

The "unsavoury spectacle of Billy Bremner running alongside a harassed referee constantly yelling in his ear" was a sight that Brian Clough cared not to witness when he was manager of Derby County, but it didn't stop him, only weeks after saying those words, from succeeding Don Revie as boss of the Leeds United team skippered by the provocative Scotsman. It wasn't exactly a ringing endorsement for the wee man, but it had not been a great week for wee men. Four days earlier, Liverpool's Kevin Keegan clocked a Kaiserslautern player diving in a pre-season friendly, and received the red card for his troubles. It could be suggested, then, that when the diminutive pair came face-to-face in a Charity Shield notable mainly for its complete absence of goodwill, neither was in the best of moods. And Keegan's demeanour certainly wasn't improved by a series of niggly tackles, culminating in a particularly nasty one from Johnny Giles which, had it connected, Keegan claimed, "would have taken my legs off". When Bremner appeared from nowhere and, in somewhat blunt terms, intimated Keegan had dived, the Liverpool player took up the challenge and swung a punch at the Leeds midfield general – and immediately copped one back. Referee Bob Matthewson couldn't believe his eyes – he had been playing cricket with Keegan only a week earlier but he had no option other than to send both packing. Yet, as if the sight of two of English football's leading lights swapping punches in the season's curtain-raiser wasn't enough, what was to follow was to etch the scene for eternity in the minds of millions who were watching live on TV: Keegan, first to the touchline, ripped off his Liverpool shirt and hurled it to the turf; Bremner, behind him, followed suit and the two, six-packs glistening in the sunshine, left a crowd behind them, mouths agape, as they strode for the tunnel.

Early Bath Temperature

 # 9/10

Bubbling. Catching up with his son in the dressing-room, Keegan's dad had to be restrained from exacting further toll on his Scottish adversary. An FA disciplinary committee, concerned about another black mark against a game riven by hooliganism, banned the pair for eleven games and fined them £500 apiece. But most interest was focused on the pair's actions in tearing off their shirts: opinion ranged from those convinced it was an act of anger to those who thought it was in shame. Keegan maintained it was neither. Bremner came to an even more unlikely conclusion: "It was a hot day and we were both annoyed," he said. "If you are hot, you take your shirt off, if you are upset you tend to do it aggressively. We didn't throw our shirts at each other."

7

Adam Parker

Hitchin Town v Aldershot. Top Field
Aldershot v Grays Athletic. The Recreation

Ground. Isthmian League premier division. September 2001

Parker, an Aldershot boy, had always wanted to play for his home-town club, but it seemed unlikely when he set off a bizarre set of expulsions for Hitchin Town in their game against the Hampshire club. Upended two minutes into the second half by a two-footed tackle, Parker was astonished to find referee Paul Vosper pointing for a free kick in the other direction. When Parker passed imprudent comment on the decision, Vosper produced the red card. Shaun Marshall followed him into the dressing-room 60 seconds later and when Matt Nolan completed the trio of malcontents, manager Andy Melvin called his players off and only the intervention of his chairman – and league chairman Alan Turvey, who was in the stand – eased the tension. But we digress: while Parker was reflecting on his actions away from the limelight, there was something else going on behind the scenes. George Borg, the Aldershot manager, had seen enough in Parker's 47-minute performance to make a £10,000 offer for his services, and Parker signed for his boyhood heroes in time for the game against Grays. But the delight he felt turned rapidly to despair as, 70 minutes into his Shots debut, he found himself making the familiar trek to the dressing-room for a foul.

Early Bath Temperature

 6/10

Familiar. Parker has the distinction of being the only player to be sent off for the same team as he was dismissed against just a week earlier.

8

Jose Antonio Chamot
Lazio v Juventus
Stadio Olimpico. Serie A. April 1998

It has been said before, but it is worth mentioning it again, if only for the benefit of players such as Jose Antonio Chamot. Referees may, depending on their mood, their modus operandi and the context, let players get away with a variety of felonies from persistent fouling to foul language, from kicking the ball away to executing the kind of dive that would beat the Chinese on the Olympics high board. But as Wayne Rooney later found out in Villarreal, there is one thing they will not abide, at any time or in any situation: sarcasm. There is not a referee on the planet who thinks it is the highest form of wit, not even Pierluigi Collina, an official who, in the present climate of media hyperbole, deferred only to God in matters of arbitration. Thus when Chamot, the Lazio defender, tried to shake Collina's hand after his team had slumped to a controversial 1-0 defeat by Juventus, the touchy Italian referee interpreted it not as the sporting gesture of a disappointed athlete, but as a thinly-disguised act of deep contempt – and sent him off.

Early Bath Temperature

2/10

Normal, since Chamot was dismissed after the final whistle. However, he still found himself in hot water with the Italian FA, who showed solidarity with their official, banning the player for an extra match after Collina had explained in his report that his behaviour had demonstrated "evident dissent".

9

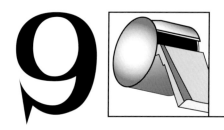

Dean Windass
Dundee United v Aberdeen
Scottish Premier League.
Tannadice. November 1997

"It's hard to bear" a local paper headline wailed over a story relating the sorry tale of the theft of a Sooty charity box from a shop in Aberdeen in November 1997. The supporters of the city's Scottish Premier League side would not have been surprised to see a similar pronouncement over the back-page stories detailing the sorry demise of their club under the stewardship of Roy Aitken. A series of home defeats came to a head when Hearts won 4-1 at Pittodrie and thousands of home fans stormed out, hurling their red and white scarves onto the pitch. A beleaguered Aitken promised to put things right for the following Saturday's fixture away to Dundee United, forcing the players to sit through a video-nasty of the Hearts defeat – but within ten seconds of the start English forward Dean Windass was booked for a foul. When, 21 minutes later, he made another bad challenge, referee Stuart Dougal decided to curtail the striker's involvement in the match. But Windass wasn't about to go quietly, and when he swore twice at Dougal, the referee showed him a second red card... and then a third, when the fuming forward ripped out a corner flag as he made his way to the dressing-room.

Early Bath Temperature

9/10

Scorching. Although, his dismissal(s) could not be blamed for the ensuing 5-0 defeat – Aberdeen were already three down by the time Windass took leave of the scene – the club fined him a fortnight's wages. But worse, when the Scottish FA slapped him with a six-game ban, it left the team with only one recognised striker for the next game – against Rangers.

10

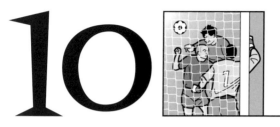

John Murray
Bury v Doncaster Rovers
Division Four. Gigg Lane. April 1973

You would have thought that when you've scored a fabulous first-half hat-trick and, with barely ten minutes of the second half gone, your team has just gone 5-0 up against rivals who have already beaten you twice that season, there would be little that could disturb your equilibrium. Not the half-hearted abuse of the dispirited travelling fans; not the niggly fouls of a demoralised opposition. Nothing, in fact, unless your name is John Murray. For what should have been a day of great celebration for the Bury winger turned sour moments after his team had notched their fifth, when he aimed one kick of his trusty right boot in the wrong direction – up Steve Uzelac's backside. The Doncaster centre-back had seen more than enough of Murray's magic for one afternoon and, probably still smarting from his wayward back-pass after 20 seconds that set up the Shakers' striker for his first, crashed into the back of him. Murray took exception to the tackle, and the short sideshow of fisticuffs that resulted from his retaliatory kick

ensured that neither player would see out the match.

Early Bath Temperature

 # 5/10

Tepid for Murray, who would have had plenty of time to reflect on his rashness. However, he didn't let it affect his touch in front of goal. After serving a three-match suspension, he returned to the team against Colchester and scored twice in a 3-0 win.

Alan Mullery
Yugoslavia v England
European Championships semi-final.
Communale Stadium. Florence. June 1968

Some notable events occurred during the 1967–68 season: Manchester United became the first English team to win the European Cup, Cardiff City reached the semi-finals of the Cup Winners Cup, and Alan Mullery became the first England player to be sent off. If the first two were significant achievements – United's win came only ten years after the Munich air disaster, and Cardiff were a struggling Second Division side who had qualified for Europe by winning the Welsh Cup – Mullery's was no mean accomplishment, either: England had played 423 matches in almost 96 years since battling for a goalless draw against Scotland at Hamilton Crescent, Glasgow in 1872, and had even won a World Cup without losing a player in this manner. Maybe it was 88 minutes of bruising Yugoslavian tackling – while England's rough-house tactics were open to view, the Balkans were more covert, applying, according to *The Times'* man on the spot, "a subtle concealment" to their foul play – but when Miljan Trivic chopped down the

Tottenham wing-half, he could take no more, kicking out and catching the Yugoslavian across the legs in return. Needless to say referee Ortiz de Menderili didn't see the original offence, and Mullery paid the price.

Early Bath Temperature

6/10

Not as cold as you'd expect. England had fallen behind to Dragan Dzajic's winning goal moments earlier, and Geoff Hurst, glad to get off the pitch, *labelled it "one of the most violent games I can remember". Even Alf Ramsey, the England manager, had sympathy for Mullery afterwards, consoling him with the opinion that nobody "if he was any sort of man" could have put up with what had been dished out to the midfielder. But England's international image was dented by the incident, and while it is not recorded whether Mullery sought absolution when the squad flew to Rome the following day to visit the Vatican, he found little forgiveness from his wife, who rang his hotel room and demanded to know why he was making such negative headlines.*

12

Unused substitute

Roy McDonagh did not expect his Colchester team, riding high in the Third Division, to be unduly tested on their visit to lowly Hereford in October 1993; in fact he was envisaging throwing a party on the bus back from Edgar Street to celebrate three points, along with his 35th birthday. But the return to Essex was to end up being anything but happy for the player-manager after a 5-0 drubbing, notable not so much for Chris Pike's hat-trick as the manner in which it was achieved: each goal was scored against a different goalkeeper. First choice John Keeley had conceded Pike's first before he came rushing out to upend Chris Fry in the 41st minute, giving away a penalty and receiving the red card from referee Ron Groves. McDonagh took over in goal himself until half-time, but the birthday boy couldn't stop Pike's spot kick, and when Pike grabbed his third, six minutes after the break, Nathan Munson, the substitute goalkeeper brought on at the interval for outfield player Steve Brown, was the man beaten. Fry had scored a fourth by the time Munson's collision with Derek Hall was deemed another offence worthy of dismissal, leaving his manager to spend the final 20 minutes in goal, plenty of time to let in Hall for the fifth and contemplate a long, pointless and most pertinently, quiet journey home.

Chapter Ten

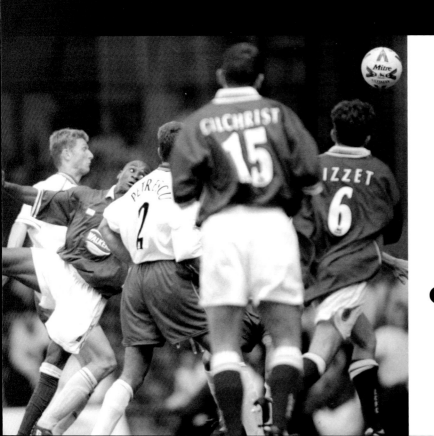

The

worst

own goals

The worst own goals

The argument for the non-existence of own goals sounds like the kind of discourse Albert Camus, the goalkeeper-cum-philosopher, would have started in the bar after turning out for the University of Algiers, but the fact of the matter is, that until a few years ago, they didn't, according to a literal reading of the rules. It seems hard to believe it but it was not until 1998, after 110 years of league football, 16 World Cups and ten European Championships, that the architects of self-inflicted misfortune were officially recognised. Law 10, on scoring, had always stated that a goal was recorded only when the ball was propelled over the line by an attacker. There was no acknowledgement of the possibility that it could be put there by an inept or unlucky member of the defending team. Did this mean, wondered a team of statisticians put on the case to revise a century of league tables, that all own goals in history would have to be declared null and void, and would there have to be wholesale redistribution of several years of Sky TV money? Unfortunately not. We have former referee Keith Cooper to thank for revealing the shocking details in an article on the FIFA website, but the world-governing body kept its nerve, sat tight and, with most of the football world still in blissful ignorance, made the subtle but necessary changes quietly and without fanfare. Which is a good thing really, because any other course of action would mean we wouldn't have been able to savour the worst this category has to offer...

1

Frank Sinclair
Arsenal v Leicester City
Highbury. and Leicester City v Chelsea
Filbert Street. the Premiership. August 1999

When news filtered through that Frank Sinclair had nodded the ball into his own net to give Chelsea an equaliser in stoppage time on the second Saturday of the 1999-2000 season, sports desks the length and breadth of the land collectively rubbed their eyes in disbelief, while Fleet Street's finest were stumped. Had not the very same Frank Sinclair done the very same thing at the very same time, against Arsenal, seven days earlier? And had not the headline writers used all the decent puns, and, in all honesty, some indecent ones – It's Frank-ly incredible, Frank's a

Bunch and Frank the Plank – on that occasion? They had. Now, left scratching their heads for further inspiration, one of them found it in the somewhat tenuous form of the popular 1970s BBC sitcom *Some Mothers Do 'Ave 'Em* and the calamitous antics of its accident-prone lead character Frank Spencer. Off-balance against his former club Chelsea, he nonetheless got his head to a cross and diverted it past Tim Flowers; that occasion? a week earlier, he had jumped to nod home a Thierry Henry header as Flowers shaped to punch it clear.

Friendly Fire

6/10

Must try harder. Despite Sinclair's finest efforts, which cost his side four points, Leicester still managed to finish the season in eighth place.

2

Rob Scott
Rotherham United v Wolves
League Cup second round.
Millmoor, October 2002

I t's bad enough scoring an own goal, but even worse when those watching fail to fully appreciate the effort that's gone into it. The reporter covering this match for the *Daily Mirror* somewhat undersold Rob Scott's contribution to the evening's entertainment, telling his readers the following morning, as something close to an afterthought, that the defender's own goal in a pulsating game "bounced in off his legs". Not only did the journalist fail to appreciate the defender's sense of timing – the score was 4-3 to Rotherham in the final minute of extra time when he struck – it also gave little credit to the skills the former Fulham striker, who had switched to the back four on his move north, had utilised in its creation.

Showing the predatory instincts that he'd failed to produce regularly enough to persuade the London club to extend his contract, Scott ensured that this League Cup tie would have to be decided on penalties when, amid a mass of players on the edge of the six-yard box, he controlled a hopeful last-ditch punt from the Wolves goalkeeper and, with the home fans screaming at him to clear it into the stands, inexplicably blasted it from close range past a perplexed Mike Pollitt in the Rotherham goal.

Friendly Fire

7/10

Minor casualties, although Scott had Denis Irwin to thank for that, the Irishman one of the guilty parties as Wolves got flustered in the shootout. Safe passage assured, Scott tried to convince anyone who'd listen that his was "a classic finish" and that "no goalkeeper in the world could have saved it", but close analysis of the video shows the mark of the failed striker – a man who can hit the target only when he's not trying to.

3

Jamie Pollock
Manchester City v QPR
Division One. Maine Road. April 1998

Not so much Pollock as pillock. The £1 million signing from Bolton was barely a month into his career with City, whose cause he had pledged to die for on putting pen to paper, when he inflicted almost terminal damage upon the relegation-threatened club. The afternoon had started positively for the home side when Georgi Kinkladze gave them the lead after only 43 seconds, but the disaster to come was presaged by the Londoners' equaliser seven minutes later, City goalkeeper Martyn Margetson picking up a back-pass from Tony Vaughan, labelled by one newspaper as "the grand master of the cock-up". Margetson handed the ball to Kevin Gallen, who simply squared to Mike Sheron to score. And it was Sheron, who took the free-kick and had started his career with City, who could claim an assist as Pollock took centre stage: intercepting a pass from the midfielder, Pollock flicked the ball up over a fellow defender and opposition forward and placed a perfect looping header over a bemused Margetson. Although City later managed to level, the two points dropped were to prove fatal.

Friendly Fire

9/10

The equivalent of dropping a live grenade among your own men, Pollock was left to reflect on "the worst moment of my career". Joe Royle, his manager, was more sanguine, accepting that with City requiring a victory from the final game at Stoke the following week to have a chance of staying up, "it is a one-game season". The one-game season proved more successful than the 45-game one that had preceded it, as City romped home 5–2, but it was too late to prevent them plummeting into Division Two.

4

Tommy Wright
Liverpool v Everton and Everton v Manchester City Division One.
Anfield and Goodison Park. March 1972

Harry Catterick's teams of the 1960s lived up to the Everton reputation for good football that had earned them the respectful epithet of the School of Science, although by 1972 the mortar board was starting to look a little crooked. With Catterick absent because of ill health, Tommy Wright, the defender with a handful of England caps to his name, began to act like an indisciplined student launching some covert research while the chemistry teacher is out of the laboratory. After diverting Kevin Keegan's cross into his own net within 35 seconds of the start of the Merseyside derby on March 4, Wright repeated the experiment under slightly different conditions a week later, when Manchester City were the visitors to

Goodison Park. This time, it seemed as if a strange form of quantum mechanics was at work as Wright dived to clear a centre after only 32 seconds, and succeeded only in sending a looping header, the arc of which would have tested the talents of a master mathematician, let alone a goalkeeper in his last season for his club, over Gordon West.

Friendly Fire

8 / 10

High casualties. Wright

added injury to the insult of the respective defeats – 4-0 to Liverpool and 2-1 to Manchester City – by dislocating his shoulder in the latter match, a mishap that put him out of action for three weeks. It was the latest instalment in the hard luck story for the full back, for 20 minutes into the season he had taken a knock that sidelined him for a lengthy period, and after a brief return had found himself looking on from the stands once more; he was making only his 13th appearance out of a possible 33 when he went down for the third time against City, and later decided to call it a day.

5

Djimi Traore
Burnley v Liverpool
FA Cup fourth round.
Turf Moor. January 2005

Many managers drive themselves almost to the brink of insanity as they try to instil in their players the need for pragmatism; time and again they will impress on a fancy-dan defender that their own penalty area is not the part of the pitch in which to win points for artistic merit. Yet, sometimes, and in spite of the bullyings and bollockings, the footballer's desire for creative expression will out. As it did for Djimi Traore on a bitter winter's night at a Turf Moor decidedly bereft of grass. Traore will, no doubt, in his younger days, have been impressed with the way that Messieurs Hansen and Lawrenson, tall, slim and well-balanced, used to ease the ball elegantly away from the edge of the box to set another flowing Liverpool move in motion. What he probably will not have seen them do, if he's totally honest, will be to collect a low cross with the daintiest of drag-backs three yards from their own goal-line on a surface more pockmarked than Luke Chadwick's face. It was subtle, it was sublime, but it was spectacularly unsuccessful and Traore's misplaced skill ended up in the back of his own net.

Friendly Fire

9/10

Court martialled. The goal was enough to send Burnley through to the next round and left Rafael Benitez to blame a "big mistake". But most journalists chose to focus not so much on Traore's error as the blunder the Liverpool manager had made in resting several first-choice players.

Harry Redknapp
Manchester United v Bournemouth
League Cup second round first leg.
Old Trafford. October 1982

Harry Redknapp's abilities were recognised at an early age, and it took all Ron Greenwood's persuasive powers to convince Harry Sr and Violet, the Poplar teenager's parents, that his future would be best served at his local club West Ham. But after seven years in the first team, he was offloaded to Bournemouth and, while on loan to Norwich, suffered the knee injury that effectively ended his playing career. Well, almost. After a spell in America and coaching at lower levels, he was taken back to Bournemouth as sideman to manager David Webb, where he was forced to make a brief comeback, five years after his last taste of senior football, because of an injury crisis. And what bigger stage to make it, after the Cherries had been drawn against one of the leading clubs in Europe. Patrolling the right flank, the natural winger showed, according to the Bournemouth evening paper, that he "could still judge a pass and pinpoint a centre". Unfortunately, he failed to judge Ashley Grimes's shot from Bryan Robson's pass, and inadvertently turned the unthreatening effort past his own goalkeeper.

Friendly Fire

5/10

Battle fatigue. Redknapp's 28th-minute error put United on the way to a fairly predictable 2-0 win, but Webb refused to blame his coach and he retained his place for the league game against Cardiff the next weekend.

7

Lee Hurst
Cambridge United v Coventry City
FA Cup third round replay.
Abbey Stadium, January 1992

There are a significant number of firsts in football that any player would be proud to have set alongside their name; first goalscorer in an FA Cup Final, first man to bag a hat-trick in a World Cup, first goalkeeper to save a penalty at Wembley. It is doubtful, however, if many would be keen to possess the one that one Coventry City defender-turned-midfielder Lee Hurst patented in injury time of what turned into a nightmarish evening in the Fens for the First Division club. Goalless, the game seemed to be heading into extra time when the Sky Blues' centre-back Andy Pearce inexplicably handled a left-wing centre from Lee Philpott. Steve Ogrizovic appeared to have rescued the situation in the short term, when he dived to produce a brilliant parry from Dion Dublin's spot-kick, but, eager to be first to the loose ball, Hurst, renowned for having a lethal left foot, used it to deadly effect as his attempted clearance speared past his goalkeeper; he was later lauded as the first player to score an own goal from a penalty.

Friendly Fire

8/10

Mishandling of explosives, but that wasn't the worst of Hurst's self-inflicted misfortunes. Leaping over a wall on the club's pre-season training excursion to an army camp, Hurst fell awkwardly and damaged knee ligaments. He never played for Coventry again.

8

Brian Gayle
Sheffield United v Leeds United
Division One, Bramall Lane, April 1992

Imagine the late Thin Lizzy lead singer Phil Lynott, then picture him after a few too many pies and you've pretty much got Brian Gayle. A man from the no-nonsense Wimbledon school of central defending, his most significant own goal before this match was when he needlessly lamped a Watford player in the quarter-finals of the 1988 FA Cup and cost himself a place in the final against Liverpool. That may have been a purely personal tragedy, but when he erred at Bramall Lane in the penultimate game of the season it was to have far wider repercussions, as unhappy Manchester United fans will tell you. With the score at 2-2, and 12 minutes left, Eric Cantona and Rod Wallace chased a bouncing ball towards the edge of the home team's penalty area. Enter Gayle, now installed as Sheffield United skipper, who took the ball down with some style on his thigh, and then spotted his injured goalkeeper hobbling towards him. He could have blasted the ball to the touchline with either foot, but instead chose the third, but least progressive, option: he panicked and looped a header over the stricken stopper, practically handing Leeds the league title.

 Friendly Fire

8/10

Worse for the Manchester United faithful. Their failure to avoid defeat at Liverpool rubber-stamped Leeds' success and Gayle confirmed his unpopularity in the Old Trafford area by signing later for Manchester City.

9

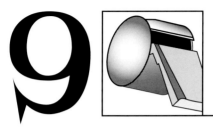

Iain Dowie
Stockport County v West Ham United
League Cup fourth round replay.
Edgeley Park. December 1996

Not surprisingly for a man with a degree in aeronautical engineering, Dowie was more than proficient in the air, although anyone stepping on to a jet he had helped to design would have been unnerved by his effort in his own penalty area against Stockport County. Like a first officer diving for Heathrow when air traffic control is lining him up for final approach into Gatwick, Dowie's radar was completely askew as he jumped unchallenged to power a first-class header past his own goalkeeper Ludek Miklosko from eight yards out. The realisation of what he had done hit him with the speed of two Pratt and Whitneys pushed to maximum thrust, and he buried his head in his hands as his team-mates gave him looks that suggested he was plain crazy. The goal levelled the scores and proved the turning point, as Second Division Stockport came from behind to reach the quarter-finals of a cup competition for the first time in 113 years.

Friendly Fire

5/10

Mid-air collision. West

Ham did not so much fade and die as crash and burn, but Dowie, who was later to limp off with a broken ankle to ironic applause from the travelling faithful, might have had some mitigation. Having failed to score in the Premiership at that point, he was obviously in need of the comfort that only the sight of a bulging net could provide, at whichever end it came.

10

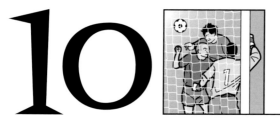

Coventry was not the first-choice settling point for Peter Ndlovu - the young Zimbabwean had always dreamed of playing for Liverpool – so when he notched what was effectively the winning goal, his first in English football, in this contest, he instead took greatest pride in the fact that he had beaten the England goalkeeper at one of the country's legendary grounds. But Ndlovu, with his 85th-minute effort, was not the only player to defeat David Seaman for the first time that afternoon – and for the other man who did, the result was not so much a dream as a complete nightmare, although it did compete with Ndlovu's effort for quality. Barely a minute had passed when Lee Dixon, the

Arsenal right-back, collected the ball on the right corner of his own 18-yard box and decided to give his goalkeeper a first touch of the ball. Without looking, he turned slightly and chipped the ball back towards Seaman, and then prepared to run towards the halfway line for the subsequent punt upfield. But stealing a look back to check on the progress of his chip, he was stunned into immobility as he watched the ball sail over the startled stopper and settle in the back of his own net.

Friendly Fire

7/10

Destruction of an arsenal, or at least a proud Arsenal record. Coventry's 2-1 victory was the home side's first defeat on their own soil in 18 months. Dixon was dragged to the post-match press conference by his sergeant major, George Graham, to explain himself, but his descriptive powers proved disappointing. "It was my first kick and I put a little extra into it," he said. "It was just an own goal."

11

Des Walker
Tottenham Hotspur v Nottingham Forest
FA Cup final, Wembley, May 1991

On the afternoon that Paul Gascoigne crocked himself when fouling Gary Charles, Paul Stewart had equalised Stuart Pearce's free kick, but Forest must have thought it was going to be their day when Gary Lineker had a goal unreasonably ruled out for offside and then missed a penalty after being brought down by Mark Crossley. Brian Clough could envisage getting his hands on a pot that had thus far eluded him. But if he was to expect the experienced men among his relatively raw troops to provide the leadership during extra time – he had chosen not to provide his men with the wisdom that had brought him League titles and

European successes before it started and chatted instead to a policeman – he was to be shaken out of that assumption by one of the most mature heads, figuratively speaking, in the business. Des Walker, the Forest and England centre-back, was a model of calm and assurance in most circumstances, and when he dived to clear Nayim's near-post corner, no-one expected anything more than another flag-kick. But Stewart, with a slight touch in front of him, rendered all calculations obsolete, and Walker headed power-fully into the roof of his own net for the Spurs winner.

 Friendly Fire

8/10

General's misjudgement. Clough was the first to offer his consolations to his mortified defender, but the damage had been done in his failure to act when his company needed him.

12

Unused substitute

Ninety minutes may not seem a formidable amount of time for someone to keep their concentration, but for underemployed goalkeepers, it can be a problem. John Burridge's answer to the quandary was to carry on a running commentary on the match from the edge of his 18-yard area, action that was sure to unnerve his defenders, if not confound opposition attackers. But even he would have found it hard to give a comprehensible description of the method in the madness of Aston Villa team-mate Chris Nicholl, one Saturday afternoon at Filbert Street in mid-March 1976. Nicholl, one of those tall, dominating centre-halves who always looked likely to pop up with crucial goals, mainly from set-pieces, did so twice to rescue a point for the relegation-threatened West Midlanders. But he would not have needed to had he not, in the first place, twice put Leicester ahead. The defender, confirming an identity crisis that had begun the week before when he turned the ball into his own net against Tottenham, beat Burridge again in the 14th minute against Leicester, before equalising just before half-time. Nine minutes into the second half, he was in the wrong place at the wrong time again, taking a centre off Robert Lee's head but only succeeding in planting his effort wide of his goalkeeper – a goal he was to consider his best of the day – before ensuring a point, and pride of place in the book of bizarre footballing feats, with his second leveller four minutes from time. The press later awarded him another first – the star rating for both Villa and Leicester – yet he remained unrepentant. "When the ball comes into the box you have got to go for it," he said. "If the worst comes to the worst I'd do the same next week." Fortunately, he appeared to have exhausted his scoring supply – the next Saturday Villa played out a goalless draw against Stoke.

Chapter Eleven

The best of
the rest of
the worsts

Worst penalty miss 1
Kevin Randall, Don Masson and Brian Stubbs Portsmouth v Notts Co.
Division Two, Fratton Park, September 1973

Confidence in their team-mates was obviously not a strong point in the Notts County side of 1973–74. Well, what other explanation could there be for a penalty, ordered to be taken three times, having to be entrusted to a different player on each occasion? You might have expected a forward of the experience of Kevin Randall, a former Bury and Chesterfield player, to have netted from a spot-kick awarded for Alan Stephenson's foul on Les Bradd, but, having seen his shot saved by John Milkins, who had moved too soon, he was not given a second chance when referee Mr Oliver ruled that it should be taken again. Up instead stepped Don Masson, a regular goalscorer from midfield, who saw his effort deflected on to the crossbar by Milkins, whose efforts again went to waste when the official indicated that Masson had shot before he had signalled his readiness – and booked him into the bargain. Attempt number three was assigned to Brian Stubbs,

but unbelievably Milkins again got enough on the ball to deflect it over. It should have proved a memorable day for the goalkeeper, the club's longest-serving player who had only returned to the first team because of an injury to Ron Tilsed, but Notts County still escaped with a 2-1 victory and Milkins was inconsolable over conceding the first goal when he failed to catch a corner.

2

Worst penalty miss 2
Billy Tunnicliffe and Jack Boothway
Colchester United v Wrexham
FA Cup second round. Layer Road. December 1947

Taking a penalty is a pressure situation, and even the finest and most skilful strikers of a ball have been found wanting by this peculiar and particular test of nerve. But few have been so overcome by the prospect that they have fainted, as opposed to feinted, as they carried out the task. One who did, however, was Billy Tunnicliffe, the Wrexham forward, as the Welsh side made an inglorious exit from the FA Cup at the hands of non-league Colchester United. The striker could claim some mitigation, having briefly fallen unconscious after he was ruthlessly cut down in the box a minute after the home side had taken the lead with an opportunist goal. But seeing no reason not to take the kick himself after coming to, he placed the ball on the spot and walked back to the end of his run-up. The start was not a problem, but as he neared the ball and shaped to pull back his leg, he veered sharply to the left, spun round in an uncontrolled manner and, according to reports at the time, nosedived sharply into the turf. The concussion victim was carted off to the dressing-room, but with a penalty still outstanding, the responsibility for concluding the drama fell to Jack Boothway. He proved equally ill-equipped to complete the mission, stubbing his toe as he tried to despatch the kick, sending the ball trickling towards goalkeeper George Wright, who was able to go down on one knee to field the effort – to the cheers of the majority of the 10,000 crowd.

3

Worst penalty miss 3
Martin Palermo
Argentina v Colombia
Copa America, Luque, Peru, July 1999

Top-class strikers are such a rare commodity – and the pressure for success so incessant – that it is not unknown for European managers to make a signing on the limited evidence of an expertly-edited showreel, especially if it is accompanied by some wily entrepreneurial patter from a widely-travelled agent promising a cut of the transfer fee. But any of those touting Martin Palermo for a multi-million-pound move from his native Argentina would have been hard-pushed to pull the wool over even the most cynical boss's eyes after their asset, nicknamed The Madman for once stripping down to his underwear and indulging in some lewd goal celebrations with a Boca Juniors team-mate, had heaped further humiliation on himself by missing three penalties during an international against Colombia. Palermo had only recently made it into Marcelo Bielsa's side, after the nation's former coach Daniel Passarella had dismissed his hopes of appearing at France 98 with the judgment that he had "no experience, no finesse and mediocre technique", and that withering assessment seemed to have some validity, as the physically imposing front-man compiled his own video nasty. His first spot-kick, after four minutes, struck the bar; the second, with 15 minutes remaining, endangered passing air traffic; and his third, in stoppage time, was placed with such delicate but barely disguised deliberation that Colombian keeper Miguel Calero almost flopped over the ball in his unnecessarily hurried attempts to keep it out. Palermo's embarrassment was shared by his countrymen, one paper writing him off as "a laughing stock who doesn't know how to kick a ball", and the value of Boca's shares plummeted nearly five per cent amid fears that any price tag on the subject of worldwide ridicule would be irrevocably damaged.

4

Worst celebration 1
Martin Palermo
Levante v Villarreal
Copa de España second round.
Estadi Ciutat de Valencia. November 2001

Palermo had his uncompromising footballing schooling at Estudiantes de La Plata, a club with a notoriously hard reputation, to thank for his ability to withstand the widespread scorn that he suffered in the wake of his Copa America disaster, and a couple of goals in Boca's 2-1 victory over Real Madrid in the Intercontinental Cup a year later helped him secure his move to Europe, where he teamed up with Villarreal in Spain. But the change of scene did not completely bring about a change of fortune: running towards the stands to lead the celebrations at his injury-time winner against Second Division Levante, he stumbled on an advertising board surrounding a small concrete wall, which collapsed under the weight of Villarreal's surging fans, breaking the tibia and fibula of his left leg. He was sidelined for two months.

Worst celebration 2
Fred Pentland
Athletic Bilbao v Europa, 1923

Long gone are the days when a goal or a victory was greeted with good old British restraint: a firm handshake or perhaps a pat on the back. Kissing and cuddling have been the custom since players started wearing perms, and the influx into the British game of foreign stars has added a further dimension: think Fabrizio Ravanelli, who kickstarted the fashion for running around with his head concealed in the hem of his shirt, or Faustina Asprilla and a nifty pas de deux with the St James's Park corner flag. Yet probably the worst celebration in football history was created by a man who travelled in the opposite direction. Fred Pentland, a centre-forward with Middlesbrough and Blackburn Rovers who was capped five times by his country, was such an English gent that he continued to wear his bowler hat when he stood on the touchline as manager of Athletic Bilbao in the early 1920s. The Basque players were so amused that whenever they won a match, they took to whipping off his headgear and ritually jumping up and down on it, until it was flattened beyond recognition. Their action gave rise to a phrase which lives on in the annals of Spanish football history. As Bilbao moved towards victory in the closing stages of a legendary cup win over Catalan club Europa in 1923, Pentland uttered the immortal words: "Que poco to quera bombin, solo tres minutos" which, roughly translated, means: "Only three more minutes left for you, bowler hat."

6

Worst hardman
Frank Barson
Barnsley, Aston Villa, Manchester United,
Watford and Hartlepool United

Frank Barson was wrought from the hardest
iron – fittingly the Yorkshireman was a
blacksmith before he turned professional
footballer with Barnsley in 1911 – but it was his
dubious team ethos that was to get him into trouble
as often as his tough-tackling style: whenever one
of his own XI was fouled he would seek out the
offender for swift retribution, often informing the
referee of his intentions first. Not surprisingly, then,
this argumentative centre- or right-half – so thick-

skinned that he once scored with a header from 30 yards, with one of those brown leather balls you see on *Antiques Roadshow* now and again, without suffering permanent brain damage – served more suspensions than any other English player, twelve in all, the last coming at his penultimate club Watford, for whom he managed only ten games after being given a seven-month ban for a sending-off at Fulham in 1928. If Barson thought he was tough, though, he was to be given a remarkable lesson in intransigence by the FA, who failed to be moved even when the Mayor of Watford delivered in person a petition from the town asking for the ban to be rescinded.

7

Worst suspension
Willie Woodburn
Rangers v Stirling Albion
Scottish League Cup first round. Ibrox Park.
August 1954

Willie Woodburn was nicknamed "Big Ben" for his imposing build, as well as his fluid movement around the field and perfect sense of timing in the tackle, for a solid Rangers defence that was referred to as the Iron Curtain. But another characteristic he shared with the famous London landmark was his tendency to get regularly wound up, and his flashpoint temper, often used to berate goalkeeper Bobby Brown when he had let in a howler, erupted once too often in a League Cup tie against Stirling Albion in 1954. He had served 14-day and 21-day bans for retaliatory punches against Motherwell in 1947, and Clyde in 1953, and later that year he was sent off for striking out at an opponent against Stirling Albion. When Rangers met Stirling again early the following season, he stepped out of line once more, responding violently to a biting challenge by Alec Patterson on an already injured knee, and this time the Scottish FA took a dimmer view, convening a disciplinary hearing and taking only four minutes to suspend the defender for a third time. For life. Tom Finney, an international opponent who Woodburn had played against during his 24-cap Scotland career, described the punishment as "a grave injustice" and although the Scottish FA revoked their decision after three years, it was too late for Woodburn – he had reached 37 and was ready to retire.

8

Worst protest
Notts County v Wednesbury Strollers
FA Cup second round. the Castle Ground.
November 1881

Disappointment in defeat is not a modern phenomenon that has come with the creation of Premierships and ever-increasing financial incentives, as the players and officials of Wednesbury Strollers, a passionate bunch despite the deceptively flippant name, would tell you if they were still around to do so. And the bare facts suggest that they had reason to feel upset after they suffered a 5-3 reverse at the hands of Notts County in the tenth year of the FA Cup. The Strollers were convinced they should have had a replay, complaining to the FA that two County goals should not have been allowed – and had only been so because the referee, L O Lindley, was from Nottingham – that the home team's full-back, H T Moore, had played under an assumed name because he was not registered, and that the crowd had at one point encroached on to the pitch and threatened them.

But that the governing body was swayed by their arguments was the least of their problems. Given the opportunity to play the match again with a neutral referee and on neutral territory, Derbyshire's county cricket ground, they probably wished they hadn't, as they slumped to a defeat about which they could have no complaints: they lost 11-1.

9 Worst match-fixing scandal
Manchester United v Liverpool
Division One. Old Trafford. April 1915

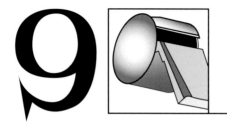

Ever since the Romans realised that they would need refreshment as they laid the stonework on their long and undeviating roads from town to town, the pub has served a central role in British life. More than just a place to drink, it has become somewhere that people gather to celebrate, where friends relax, colleagues 'talk shop' – and football players fix the result of a crucial Easter fixture. Yes, for it was in the dark and dingy recesses of Manchester's Dog & Partridge a few months after the outbreak of the First World War, that several players from Manchester United and Liverpool arranged that United, facing relegation, would beat the Merseysiders, comfortably in mid-table, 2-0. Suspicions were first aroused when Patrick O'Connell,

United's Irish international, missed a penalty by an unfeasibly wide margin, and were heightened by Liverpool's strange reluctance to attack. But it was only when Fred Pagnam almost pulled a goal back in the last minute – he hit the bar and was given a furious dressing-down by his team-mates for nearly rendering the agreement void – that observers realised something really was amiss. The FA ordered an investigation, and a commission found that the game had been fixed 'for the purposes of betting and winning considerable sums of money'. That footballers 'dependent on the game for their livelihoods should resort to such base tactics' was incredible, it said. But it was not looking at the wider picture: many influential people were calling for the abandonment of the game during the war, and the players were only trying to make a bob or two before they were mown down in the trenches. Nine were suspended, and because the clubs themselves were found to have played no part in the arrangement and escaped sanction, United survived by an ill-gained point – sending Chelsea down.

10

Worst gamesmanship
Wrexham v Lincoln City
Division Three North.
Racecourse Ground. April 1927

The afternoon of April 9, 1927, was decidedly unspringlike. We are not talking a little bit parky here, a little bit showery there: we are talking rain, a wind of almost hurricane intensity and the sort of serious cold that reminds brass monkeys to afford adequate protection to their privates before venturing out, not to mention threatening to decimate the football programme. Yet a saturated Racecourse Ground had been passed as playable, and Lincoln City were obliged to fulfil the fixture after travelling across the country. And if they were not happy bunnies at the outset, when they emerged for the second half 2-0 down and in their still-sodden garments to see the home side lining up in a dry, freshly-laundered, and neatly-ironed new kit, they bore the mood of Watership Down blighted by an outbreak of myxomatosis. Action was required, and their first attempt to force an abandonment, launching the ball over the stands at every opportunity, only irritated the small crowd while having no effect on a referee showing perfect synchronicity with the poor weather theme by rejoicing in the name of Mr Fogg.

It became clear that another strategy was called for, and it took shape when the Lincoln trainer, called on to administer treatment to one player who had mysteriously collapsed as he went to take a throw-in, handed around a restorative bottle of liquid to several more team-mates. When three of them slumped to their knees grasping their stomachs in agony, Fogg saw little suspicious in the situation, and called the game off with 15 minutes left. A protest by Wrexham fans failed to influence the FA, who ordered the match to be replayed, and three weeks later Lincoln returned to grab a 1–1 draw.

11

Worst curse

Andarai v Vasco de Gama
Brazilian Championship. December 1937

Touching the *This is Anfield* sign, putting the left boot on first or being the last player out on to the pitch, British footballers have their superstitions, most of which are relatively harmless. But in some countries their significance is much greater. In Africa, for example, it's not the quality of your striker that's all important, but the quality of your witch doctor; in fact, so successful are some medicine men that it's surely only a matter of time before Jonathan Barnett or Pini Zahavi signs them up for a lucrative move to Europe. And, if they're not always on top of their game – one erred badly when he ordered his midfield quartet to urinate in the opposition's goalmouth prior to the second half, and earned them a life ban – it beats the piping out of a marching band and majorettes for pre-match entertainment. South

American football also regularly dances to the rhythm of the supernatural, and it is in Brazil that what is probably football's worst curse scenario evolved. Vasco de Gama, one of the country's leading clubs, were on their way to play Andarai when their bus collided with a lorry, delaying their arrival. Andarai could have claimed the points, but waited until Vasco, much the stronger team, turned up, on the condition that Vasco went easy on them. But when the visitors failed to keep to their side of the bargain, romping to a 12-0 victory, Arubinha, the Andarai coach, knelt down and enjoined the spirits to make sure Vasco went without a championship for 12 years – a year for every goal. The curse was confirmed, according to legend, by his burial of a frog – the conduit for the standard Brazilian jinx – under the Vasco stadium. The Vasco team laughed it off, but they had had enough by the time the trophy cabinet had remained bare for seven years, and dug up the whole pitch in a desperate, but vain, search for the ill-starred amphibian. Finally, Arubinha relented, admitted there was no frog, and lifted the curse – and the next season, Vasco won the championship.

Selected Bibliography

General

Phil Ball: Morbo, The Story of Spanish Football, *WSC Books, 2003*

Alex Belios: Futebol, The Brazilian Way of Life, *Bloomsbury, 2003*

Mihir Bose: Sports Babylon, *Carlton Books, 1999*

David Conn, Chris Green, Richard McIlroy and Kevin Mousley: Football Confidential 2, Scams, Scandals and Screw Ups, *BBC Worldwide, 2003*

Eduardo Galeano: Football in Sun and Shadow, *Fourth Estate, 1997*

Ulrich Hesse-Lichtenberger: Tor! The Story of German Football, *WSC Books, 2003*

Christov Ruhn (editor): Le Foot, The Legends of French Football, *Abacus, 2000*

Chris Taylor: The Beautiful Game, A Journey Through Latin American Football, *Phoenix Paperbacks, 1998*

Gordon Thomson: The Man in Black, A History of the Football Referee, *Prion Books, 1998*

Russ Williams: Football Babylon 2, *Virgin Books, 1998*

Bob Wilson: You've Got To Be Crazy, On Goalkeepers and Goalkeeping, *Weidenfeld and Nicolson, 1989*

Biographies/ Autobiographies

John Barnes (with Henry Winter): The Autobiography, *Headline, 2000*

David Elleray: The Man in the Middle, *Time Warner Books, 2004*

Barry Fry (with Phil Rostron): Big Fry, Riotous Tales from a Larger than Life Football Manager, *Collins Willow, 2000*

Paul Gascoigne (with Hunter Davies): Gazza, My Story, *Headline, 2004*

Vinnie Jones: Vinnie, The Autobiography, *Headline, 1998*

Denis Law: The King, Bantom Press, *2003*

Diego Maradona: El Diego, the Autobiography of the World's Greatest Footballer, *Yellow Jersey Press, 2004*

Stuart Pearce (with Bob Harris): Psycho, The Autobiography, *Headline, 2000*

Harry Redknapp (with Derek McGovern): 'Arry, *Collins Willow, 1999*

Nobby Stiles (with James Lawton): After the Ball, My Autobiography, *Coronet, 2003*

Jack Taylor (with David Jones): Jack Taylor, World Soccer Referee, *Pelham Books, 1976*

Stan Ternent (with Tony Livesey): Stan the Man, A Hard Life in Football, *John Blake, 2004*

Alan Wilkie (with George Miller): One Night at the Palace, A Referee's Story, *The Parrs Wood Press, 2002*

Statistics/Factual

Bryon Butler: The Football League 1888-1988, the Official Illustrated History, *Queen Anne Press, 1988*

Mike Collett: The Complete Record of the FA Cup, *SportsBooks Ltd, 2003*

Maurice Golesworthy: The Encyclopaedia of Association Football, *Robert Hale Books, November 1969*

Barry J Hugman: Football League Players' Records 1946-1988, *The Arena Press, 1988*

Simon Inglis: The Football Grounds of England and Wales, *Collins Willow, 1983*

Michael Joyce: Football League Players' Records 1888-1939, *SoccerData, 2004*

Ivan Ponting: The FA Cup Final, A Post-War History, Tony Williams Publications, 1993

David Prole (compiler): Funny Game Football: Curiosities, Coincidences, Statistics and Other Soccer Trivia, *1990*

Jack Rollin: Soccer Shorts, *Guinness, 1989*

Graham Sharpe: The Book of Bizarre Football, *Robson Books, 2000*

Club histories etc.

Stuart Basson: Chesterfield FC, the official history 1867-2000, *Yore Publications, 2000*

Tony Brown: Notts County, the official history 1862-1995, *Yore Publications, 1996*

Harry Glasper: Middlesbrough, a complete record, *Breedon Books, 1989*

Ramon Melcom, Stratton Smith (editors): The Real Madrid Book of Football, *Souvenir Press, 1961*

Tony Matthews: Who's Who of Aston Villa, *Mainstream Publishing, 2004*

Ken Smales: Forest, the first 125 Years, *Temple Printing, 1991*

Newspapers, magazines and periodicals

The Times, The Independent, The Guardian, The Sun, The Daily Record, The Glasgow Herald, Leicester Mercury, East Anglian Daily Times, Colchester Express, Hull Daily Mail, Yorkshire Post, York Evening Press, Wrexham Leader, Burnley News, Northern Echo, Teesside Gazette, Aldershot News, Bury Times, Liverpool Echo, Nottingham Evening Post, Birmingham Evening Mail, Portsmouth News, Southern Evening Echo, Aberdeen Press and Journal, Aberdeen Evening Express, The Sporting Mirror, Four Four Two, Total Football